TEACH YOURSELF BOOKS

MANAGEMENT ACCOUNTING

The role of the Management Accountant is to present management, i.e. the decision makers, with the best possible financial information upon which they can base their decisions, and also to establish control systems to ensure that the best use is being made of the concern's resources—men, machines, materials and money.

This book sets out the main systems and techniques which are at present available to the management accountant to enable him to fulfil this role. Topics covered are: Historical and Standard Costing, Budgetary Control, Financial Planning, Marginal Costing and Decision Information.

TEACH YOURSELF BOOKS

MANAGEMENT ACCOUNTING

B. MURPHY
A.I.M.T.A., D.M.A., A.M.B.I.M.

*Principal Lecturer in Management Accounting,
Huddersfield Polytechnic*

TEACH YOURSELF BOOKS
ST. PAUL'S HOUSE   WARWICK LANE   LONDON EC4

First printed 1970

Copyright © 1970
The English Universities Press Ltd.

ISBN 0 340 12495 4

Printed in Great Britain for
The English Universities Press Ltd.,
by Richard Clay (The Chaucer Press), Ltd.,
Bungay, Suffolk

ACKNOWLEDGEMENTS

I wish gratefully to acknowledge the help and assistance given by David Lester, A.I.M.T.A., A.C.W.A., who painstakingly read each chapter and provided me with invaluable criticisms and comments for improving the original text.

I should also like to express my thanks to the Institute of Cost and Works Accountants for granting permission to quote from their booklet *Terminology of Cost Accounting* and also to the Centre for Interfirm Comparison which provided me with a wealth of information on its work.

My thanks are also due to Catherine McLester for the expert way in which she translated my unintelligible writing into typescript and to my wife Barbara for the help and encouragement which she has given me in the preparation of this book.

TO
BARBARA

CONTENTS

CONTENTS

Chapter 1

INTRODUCTION

What is Management Accounting?

The term is defined by the Institute of Cost and Works Accountants in their publication *Cost Terminology* as "the presentation of accounting information in such a way as to assist management in the creation of policy and in the day-to-day operation of an undertaking". From this definition it will be appreciated that there is a distinction to be drawn between the management accountant and the financial accountant, but this distinction should not lead to two separate and distinct fields of accounting with no inter-relationships.

It is not possible for the accountant to work in isolation and he must have a working knowledge of the many other fields which affect the business organisation. Such knowledge will cover the fields of economics, law, management, statistics and psychology. He should be able to apply his knowledge of these subjects to his own particular area of accountancy. Economics, for example, will help to explain to the accountant what determines prices and what is likely to be the optimum output for his particular organisation, why interest rates change, etc. He must also remember that *people* are responsible for making decisions and incurring costs; and a knowledge of psychology will help him to understand why certain actions are followed, particularly in cases where the most economical policies are not always pursued. For instance, an owner may be prepared to forfeit maximising profits in order to be able to locate his business in an area which gives him personal satisfaction. The accountant's role as information manager will also bring him into constant contact with *people* either seeking information from him or depending upon him to interpret it for them, and it is essential that in this role he contributes to the efficient operation of the organisation and avoids creating conflicts. He should appreciate, however, that his training is primarily as an accountant and if he requires advice on economics, law, etc., he should take his problem to the specialist in these fields.

In his capacity as information manager he will collect and produce information for three broad purposes:

(a) for use by management within the organisation to plan and control current operations and future short-term operations;

(b) to enable management to make special decisions and formulate long-term plans, e.g. capital investment decisions;

(c) to report historical information to interested outside bodies such as shareholders and the Inland Revenue.

This last aspect is generally known as financial accounting, and its main aim is to present a true and fair view of the financial affairs of the organisation. This aim will apply just as much to the non-profit-making organisations such as local authorities and charities as to the business enterprise. The main documents used to show this information will be the Trading and Profit and Loss Account and the Balance Sheet, together with the Directors' and Auditors' reports. The preparation and presentation of these documents will follow established principles, some of which have been embodied in such major Acts as the Companies Acts 1948 and 1967 in the United Kingdom. The majority of these principles are, however, based on the recommendations of the various accountancy bodies such as the American Institute of Certified Public Accountants and the Association of Certified and Corporate Accountants. It should be noted that these are only recommendations and they are not binding on members: obviously, however, such bodies are constantly developing improved ways of presenting financial information and to follow the accepted principles will usually mean that the best available procedures are being adopted. However, individual cases call for individual action and a certain amount of flexibility in applying these principles may be necessary.

The presentation of this *historical* information is a very necessary task. It must be remembered that the shareholders of a company are the owners of that company and the directors are managing the company on their behalf. It is essential that periodical reports of the directors' stewardship should be given to the owners. This information is conventionally given in full once a year, with interim reports being made during the course of that year. This enables the shareholders to judge whether the performance of the company in the past twelve months has been satisfactory. From their standpoint this usually means that sufficient profits have been made to give them an adequate return on their investment. It also allows some assessment of the future prospects of the company to be formed. The Inland Revenue will be equally concerned with the performance of the concern for the past twelve months in order to ensure that a correct assessment is made of the tax liability of the concern on its trading activities for the period.

The whole outlook of the financial accountant will be seen to be concerned with historical information and is based on the static concept of yearly accounting. In a going concern the normal state is dynamic, not static. This is best illustrated by the Balance Sheet which presents a picture of the concern on one particular day, e.g. the 31st December each year. It will be apparent that the whole picture presented by this statement may well have been changed the following day. New assets may have been purchased, creditors may have been paid, debtors may have been raised and stock reduced, to give but a few examples of the normal day-to-day activities which will affect figures shown on the Balance Sheet. Another point is that the compilation of these statements takes time and it may even be months later when the Final Accounts, as they are called, are presented for external inspection. Attempts may be made to overcome this time-lag by presenting accounts more frequently, e.g. once a month, but this involves many problems of valuation of assets and liabilities and apportionment of expenses. Although they are a step in the right direction even these monthly statements usually take a week or more to prepare, which means again that the facts are out of date by the time they are considered.

Another limiting factor of financial accounting is that the accounts show the overall trading picture of the concern for a particular period. It is not possible to ascertain from such accounts whether the concern is pursuing its most profitable lines of business or what the cost of operating a department is, or whether the most effective use is being made of materials, labour and machines. Accounts usually cover a period of twelve months (the period used also for taxation calculations), but the trade cycle of the business may be more or less than twelve months. Such differences can be overcome by the use of management accounting techniques. Consider the following illustration.

The financial accounts of a company show the following position:

Trading Account

	£		£
Materials used	15,000	Sales	50,000
Wages	25,000		
Gross profit on trading			
(20%) c/d	10,000		
	£50,000		£50,000

Profit and Loss Account

	£		£
Administration expenses	3,000	Gross profit b/d	10,000
Selling expenses	1,500		
Distribution expenses	500		
Net profit (10%)	5,000		
	£10,000		£10,000

It will be seen that the company appears to have made a satisfactory profit for the year of £5,000, which represents 10% of the turnover, i.e. sales. However, if the figures are analysed into the products which are made, the contribution which each makes to this 10% can be established.

Let us assume that the company deals with three products, A, B and C.

An analysis of the costs and income reveals the following:

	Total £	Products A £	B £	C £
Materials used	15,000	6,000	4,000	5,000
Wages	25,000	10,000	7,000	8,000
	40,000	16,000	11,000	13,000
Administration expenses	3,000	1,300	800	900
Selling expenses	1,500	800	300	400
Distribution expenses	500	300	100	100
Total expenses	45,000	18,400	12,200	14,400
Sales	50,000	23,000	11,000	16,000
Profit	5,000	4,600	—	1,600
Loss	—	—	1,200	—
Percentage of sales	10%	20%	—	10%

These detailed allocation accounts reveal that only product C is earning the same profit percentage as revealed by the financial statement. Product A is earning 20% on turnover and product B is incurring a £1,200 loss during the period. Obviously it should be possible to improve the overall profitability of the concern by directing attention to product B. This might be achieved by (i) ceasing to produce it, (ii) increasing advertising on it, (iii) ensuring that allocations of overheads, etc., are fair to it. It may be that product B is a by-product which helps maintain the labour force and is therefore a necessary expense. Whatever the reason for this loss it should be investigated and the facts placed before the management to enable them to take a decision on the future of product B.

This type of statement will be prepared by the cost accountant, but if he is producing his information in accordance with purpose (a) outlined earlier (p. 2), i.e. to enable management to plan and control current operations, action should have been taken at an early stage to correct the position which is revealed above.

The management accountant deals with the present and the future rather than the past. His role is to help management to fulfil the objectives of the business. These objectives, incidentally, are not covered by the general statement that a concern is in business to make a profit. Obviously unless it is able to make an adequate return on its endeavours it will not stay in that particular business; but the objectives of a business also include the reason for the business existing—e.g. to make motor-cars or electric kettles or pot plants. The management accountant presents management (i.e. the decision makers) with the best possible financial information upon which they can base their decisions, and he also establishes control systems to ensure that the best use is being made of the concern's resources, i.e. men, machines, materials and money.

The main systems and techniques which are at present available to the management accountant to enable him to achieve these aims will be considered in subsequent chapters. The main framework consists of:

Historical Costing. This is concerned with actual costs which have been incurred. Although these are of limited value (see above), they are essential in order to operate a standard costing system.

Standard Costing. This involves setting up pre-determined standards for costs, actual costs then being compared with the standards and the differences, i.e. variances, analysed and reasons sought for them.

Budgetary Control. Plans are prepared for a future period in financial terms. This ensures that responsibilities for expenditure and revenue are established and a continuous comparison may then be made of the actual with the budgeted figures, to enable the differences to be analysed into the controllable and the uncontrollable. Suitable corrective action can then be taken as soon as necessary.

Financial Planning. This will cover the various methods available to finance the business, and the importance of working capital. The source and application of funds will also be considered together with the value of accounting ratios and inter-firm comparisons.

Marginal Costing. This involves first the division of costs into fixed and variable, and second the effect on profit of changes in the volume or type of output. Only costs which vary with production are charged to the operations, fixed costs being written off to profits in the period in which they arise.

Decision Information. The accountant should be in a position to present management with the financial implications of alternative schemes, e.g. to make a product or buy it from outside suppliers. Capital investment decisions may similarly be subject to the scrutiny of the accountant using such techniques as discounted cash flow in order to assess the real value of alternative proposals and to ensure that an adequate return is being obtained on the capital employed in the business. Problems of maintaining the capital of the concern in periods of continuing inflation will also be of concern to the accountant, although as outlined later in Chapter 12 these problems have only recently concerned the majority of accountants and few companies have yet formulated a satisfactory policy to help solve such problems.

Questions

1. What is management accounting?

2. What are the three broad purposes for which the accountant produces information?

3. Which three statements does the financial accountant use to present his historical information?

4. Explain the limitations of the balance sheet.

5. Is it possible to ascertain from the financial accounts whether a business is pursuing its most profitable line of business?

6. Who will usually be responsible for preparing a detailed break-down of costs and sales, over products?

7. What is the role of the management accountant in the organisation?

8. Name the four resources of a business which management should make sure are being fully used.

9. Outline the purpose of budgetary control.

10. What type of decision will be subject to the technique of discounting cash flows?

Chapter 2

FUNDAMENTALS OF ACCOUNTING

In order to appreciate fully the role of management accounting in the business organisation it is necessary to have some knowledge of the basic concepts of accounting, and this chapter will be devoted to a discussion of these concepts.

Let us consider how an individual might show his financial position at a particular date. He would probably first consider what his assets are and then offset these with his liabilities: this would leave him with a sum which might be said to represent his net worth.

Consider the following figures which might represent the position of Mr. Average:

Assets

	Owned 31st December
	£
House	6,500
Car	700
Furniture	1,500
Caravan	400
Building Society deposit	500
Investment in Unit Trusts	200
	£9,800

Some of these assets are not fully owned by Mr. Average and the amount owed must be shown as a liability.

Liabilities and Claims

	31st December
	£
Mortgage on house	4,500
Bank loan on car—outstanding	350
Hire purchase on furniture	500
Bank overdraft	100
Total liabilities	5,450
Net worth or owner's capital	4,350
	£9,800

Not all Mr. Average's assets and liabilities are listed here. He may, for example, be married with two children and he may have some difficulty in deciding which side of his balance sheet these should appear—whether as assets or as liabilities. The major difficulty would, however, be to put a money value on such items; and for this reason items requiring a subjective assessment of their worth are usually not included.

These two statements show the assets which Mr. Average owns and the way in which they have been or are being financed. It will be seen that the total of the assets agrees with the total of the liabilities and claims, but this does not mean that the figures in the statements must be correct just because they "balance". We have in fact balanced the liabilities statement by showing the difference between the liabilities and the assets as the owner's capital. If the asset values were to remain unchanged and were fully owned by Mr. Average the balance sheet would look like this:

	Assets		Claims
	£		£
House	6,500	Owner's capital	9,800
Car	700		
Furniture	1,500		
Caravan	400		
Building Society deposit	500		
Unit Trusts	200		
	£9,800		£9,800

The balance sheet still "balances" at £9,800, but now all the assets are fully paid for and the owner's capital is increased from the previous figure of £4,350 to £9,800.

The balance sheet of a business will contain the same basic information as the balance sheet of Mr. Average, but because of the more complex nature of a business undertaking the list of assets and liabilities is likely to be longer and more detailed. The main items which appear in a business balance sheet are shown below:

Assets

Fixed

Land and buildings
Plant and machinery
Fixtures and fittings
Motor vehicles

Current

Stocks of raw materials
Work in progress
Debtors
Cash at bank
Cash in hand

The claims or sources of capital which relate to these assets are usually classified on a time basis, i.e. long-term, medium-term and short-term.

Claims and Liabilities

Permanent or Long-Term

Share capital
   Ordinary shares
   Preference shares
Retained profits

Medium-Term

Loan capital
Debentures (Mortgages)

Short Term

Bank overdraft
Creditors

Once again the totals of these two statements will "balance".

We are now in a position to consider the accountancy equation and the meaning of double-entry accounting. It is interesting to note that the double-entry system, which results in a balance sheet "balancing", was in use as long ago as the thirteenth century and was developed by the merchants of Italy of that period. A perfect set of books on the double-entry principle is in existence which dates from 1340 and records the affairs of Marsan of Genoa.

The basic equation is:

$$\text{Assets} = \text{Liabilities} + \text{Shareholders' equity}$$
$$\;\;(A)\qquad\qquad(L)\qquad\qquad\qquad(SE)$$

Shareholder's equity is made up of the original capital which has been subscribed by the shareholders plus profits which have been retained in the business for future activities but which could have been paid out to the shareholders as dividends.

The equation could therefore be written as:

$$A = L + \text{Shareholders' capital} + \text{Retained profits}$$

A profit arises when the total revenue during the period exceeds the total expenses incurred in that period. If we say that none of the profit was paid out as a dividend, i.e. all the profit was retained in the business, then the equation may be written:

$$A = L + \text{Shareholders' capital} + \text{Total revenue}$$
$$- \text{Total expenses}$$

Transposing gives us:

$$A + \text{Total expenses} = L + \text{Shareholders' capital} + \text{Revenue}$$

The left-hand side of the equation = the right-hand side.

If left-hand side is represented by DEBIT and right-hand side by CREDIT, then DEBIT = CREDIT.

The recording of total revenue and total expenses takes place in individual accounts which at the end of the accounting period are brought together in the Trading and Profit and Loss Account. If there has been a satisfactory trading period, then the subsequent profit will increase the shareholders' equity by increasing the retained earnings figure. If, on the other hand, a loss has been made then this will reduce the Shareholders' equity.

It is important to realise that the retained earnings do not represent a pot of cash which the shareholders might claim at any time. It would be very wasteful if this were the case as cash in itself earns nothing and the business must use any available cash to purchase revenue earning assets or reduce its liabilities.

To illustrate the point in the previous paragraph let us see what happens to the original cash which the owner of a business initially puts up. The opening balance sheet would look like this:

	£		£
Cash	1,000	Owner's capital	1,000

He now purchases certain equipment which costs £400. After this transaction the balance sheet would be:

	£		£
Cash	600	Owner's capital	1,000
Equipment	400		
	£1,000		£1,000

The cash has been reduced by the £400 paid for the equipment and this equipment is now shown in the balance sheet as an asset.

Let us assume that the rest of the cash is spent on stock. The balance sheet would now look like this:

	£		£
Cash	Nil	Owner's capital	1,000
Equipment	400		
Stock	600		
	£1,000		£1,000

If the stock is sold, say for £800, then this will mean a reduction of the stock figure to nil, an increase in the cash figure to £800, and the difference between the cost of the stock and the revenue from selling it, i.e. £200 represents the profit earned on the transaction and in balance sheet terms will be shown as retained earnings:

	£		£
Cash	800	Owner's capital	1,000
Equipment	400	Retained earnings	200
Stock	Nil		
	£1,200		£1,200

The owner may now decide to buy the same amount of stock and to use the other £200 of cash to buy some new equipment. After these transactions have taken place the balance sheet would be:

	£		£
Cash	Nil	Owner's capital	1,000
Equipment	600	Retained earnings	200
Stock	600		
	£1,200		£1,200

It will be seen that the retained earnings are now represented by assets other than cash, i.e. either by equipment or stock. It would not be possible for the owner suddenly to decide to take out of the business the retained earnings, as they are represented by assets which are not easily divisible.

The double-entry system requires that for each debit entry in an account there must be a corresponding credit entry in some other account. For each item in the balance sheet there will be a separate account. In addition there will be numerous accounts recording revenues received and expenses incurred during the period. At the end of the period these are totalled and any balance on the account is taken to the Trading or Profit and Loss Account, which itself forms part of the double-entry system.

We will work through a simple practical example to illustrate these points.

The opening balance sheet of J. Bloggs at 1st January is shown in the first column. During the year the following transactions took place:

1. £300 of stock was purchased for cash. (This will increase the stock figure by £300 and reduce the cash by £300.)

2. New equipment costing £400 was purchased, the seller agreeing to a sale on "credit terms". (This will increase the equipment account by £400 and increase the liabilities under the heading creditors by £400.)

3. Stock was sold for £200 cash, the original cost being £150. (This will decrease the stock by £150,

increase the cash by £200 and increase the retained earnings or profits by £50.)

4. A debtor pays his account which is for £200. (The cash will be increased by £200 and debtors reduced by £200.)

5. Payments totalling £250 were made to creditors. (This will reduce cash by £250 and reduce creditors by £250.)

6. Stock was sold for £300, on credit terms, the original cost being £200. An invoice was sent to the buyer. (Stock is reduced by £200, debtors are increased by £300 and retained earnings are increased by £100.)

Consider the account of J. Bloggs shown below.

J.

	1st Jan. £	Assets 1	2	3	4	5	6	31st Dec. £
Fixed Assets								
Land and building	2,000							2,000
Furniture and equipment	1,500		+400					1,900
Current Assets								
Stock	400	+300		−150			−200	350
Debtors	250				−200		+300	350
Cash	350	−300		+200	+200	−250		200
	£4,500	Nil	+400	+50	Nil	−250	+100	£4,800

Note: Retained earnings are equivalent to profits retained.

It will be seen that after the dual aspect of each transaction has been recorded the left-hand side, i.e. the debit side still equals the right-hand side, i.e. the credit side. The balance is either nil as in the case of items 1 and 4, or a sum which shows a change in balance on at least two accounts.

It should be mentioned that a balance sheet when used in its proper function is not part of the double-entry system but just shows the balances which are standing on those accounts which have not been closed off for the period and carried to the Trading and Profit and Loss Account. It is usual to show the Assets on the right-hand side of the balance sheet and claims and liabilities on the left-hand side. This ensures that a distinction is drawn between the actual accountancy system in operation and this statement of the position of a business on one particular day, which is called the balance sheet.

Accounting is an art rather than an exact science and in order to ensure some uniformity in the system of accounting it is necessary to have certain generally accepted guide-lines which are capable of formulating a basic framework in which the system can work. Without such guide-lines the whole art of accounting would flounder and no party either internal or external would be able to place any reliance on the results shown by the accountant.

Bloggs

	1st Jan. £	Claims and Liabilities 1	2	3	4	5	6	31st Dec. £
Owner's capital	4,000							4,000
Retained earnings	200			+50			+100	350
Current Liabilities								
Creditors	300		+400			−250		450
	£4,500	Nil	+400	+50	Nil	−250	+100	£4,800

The main guide-lines are outlined below:

(a) *The Entity Concept.* Each business, whether it is run by one man or by a partnership or as a limited company, is regarded as a separate entity and accounts are kept for each entity. This means that in the one-man business it is necessary to distinguish between the individual as an individual and the individual as owner of the business. We can illustrate this point by considering the man who owns a grocery store. Let us assume that his business balance sheet shows his equity (i.e. his original capital plus retained profits) to be standing at £1,000 and that his stock figure is shown at £200. Now consider that he wishes to use some of his stock for his own family. Say this stock has a value of £20. From our previous discussion of double-entry accounting we know that two accounts must be affected by this transaction. The stock figure is going to be reduced by £20, but where is the other entry to be made? There are two solutions, both of which show how the business transactions must be kept separate from the owner's private transactions.

The first solution would be for the owner to treat the stock as being sold to him just as it might have been sold to a customer. He will then, as the customer would, pay for the stock in cash, i.e. out of his own pocket into the till. The second and more usual solution would be to reduce the owner's equity by the cost of the stock, so that the equity would now be £980 and the stock £180. In the case of a limited company, the company has a separate legal entity from the shareholders who own it and it is fairly easy to distinguish between the transactions of each.

(b) *The Going Concern Concept.* This concept presumes that the business is treated as a continuing entity, so that valuations of assets, etc., are based on the assumption that they will be used to help produce further goods or will be sold in the normal course of trading. Otherwise the accountant would have to try to value assets on the basis of the business closing down tomorrow, which under normal circumstances would be unrealistic, and would require many subjective decisions. Machinery, for example, which might be in good condition but only capable of producing a certain product manufactured by the business would have no value, if account had to be taken of what the position would be if the business was closed down next day. If, however, the business is viewed as a going concern the machine is a valuable asset capable of earning revenue for the business in future years, and a monetary value should be placed on it.

(c) *Measurement is in Money Terms.* The accountant deals only in those facts which can be reduced to monetary terms. The balance sheet shows in monetary terms certain facts relating to assets of the business and the various claims, again in monetary terms, against these assets. It will not reveal facts which may have a very important bearing on the future of the business but which are not capable of being reduced to the common denominator of money, e.g. that relations with the unions are strained, or that a large quantity of plant is likely to become obsolete in the next six months because of a new invention.

(d) *Stable Monetary Unit.* It is generally accepted that objective evidence should be the accounting basis for recording transactions. This involves valuing the resources of a business at cost or market price, whichever is the lower. It does mean that the balance sheet of a business cannot be used as a measure of the current worth of that business, particularly when there is an unstable currency which, because of inflation, is constantly being devalued in real terms. The main reason against making up-to-date assessments of current values is, once again, the subjective nature of such assessments and the lack of reliable information about price changes on which assessments could be made. As a compromise, when it is obvious that an asset has increased in value (e.g. land), a number of companies have undertaken a revaluation of the asset and made the appropriate adjustments in the balance sheet.

(e) *Realisation Concept.* Revenues should not be recorded until they are realised, but losses should be recorded even though they may not yet have occurred. This is the conservative approach which has an important influence on the accountant when he is recording transactions. In connection with the sale of some commodity the accountant would only take account of the sale when the goods were delivered to the buyer. No income would be shown throughout the stages necessary to get the goods into a saleable state, despite the fact that money had been spent on the processes.

The main exception to this is in the case of long-term contracts such as shipbuilding, where it is prudent to show a proportion of the revenue each year to avoid violent fluctuations from year to year. Again, however, the recorded income would be conservatively estimated, and might be three-quarters of what had actually been earned during the period from the work done.

(f) *Expenses are Matched with Revenues.* Costs should be matched with the revenue which they earn. Once the accounting period has been settled (e.g. twelve months), all costs incurred in earning the revenue received during that period should be shown. These costs may have occurred in past years (e.g. the purchase of plant and equipment), or the present year (e.g. wages), or will occur in cash in a future year (e.g. rent which is paid in arrears).

Items which have not been fully used in earning the revenue of the period will be shown in the balance sheet as assets. In this respect they represent stored-up costs which will be used to produce future revenues and will be set against such revenues when they are used.

(g) *Consistency.* The statements prepared by the accountant must be consistent from period to period. The same methods of valuation must be employed from year to year for the results to be meaningful; and the accounts should not be manipulated to provide a desired result which would be inconsistent with previous procedures adopted. This does not, of course, mean that no changes should ever take place, but changes should be infrequent and should be clearly noted on the relevant statements.

Questions

1. If Assets are £10,000, what is the total of Claims and Liabilities?
2. If Assets are £10,000 and Liabilities £4,000, what are the owner's claims?
3. Draft a balance sheet of a Company showing the usual Assets and Claims and Liabilities which might be included.
4. Write out the accountancy equation.
5. Explain the meaning of debit and credit.
6. Are retained earnings usually kept in the form of cash or are they utilised to purchase new assets, etc.?
7. Explain what you understand by the expression "dual aspect of each transaction".
8. What do you understand by the going concern concept?
9. The accountant deals only in facts which can be reduced to monetary terms. What other facts might have an effect on the future of the business?
10. Explain what is meant by the realisation concept.

Chapter 3

FINANCING THE BUSINESS

Whatever the type of business organisation, e.g. sole trader, partnership or limited company, it will require initial capital to enable it to commence its operations and no doubt additional capital as its activities expand. There are a number of ways in which this capital can be raised, and with ever-increasing interest rates it is essential that all possible means should be considered before the final source or sources are chosen.

The initial capital requirements will be based on a capital budget. The purpose of the capital budget is to estimate the expenditure which is likely to be incurred in establishing the business, including the initial asset requirements such as land, buildings, plant and machinery; preliminary expenses, e.g. legal fees, issuing house fees, and also the amount needed to finance the actual production until income from initial sales is received. The capital budget may be a complicated document if we are considering a medium-size company, or just a simple statement if the needs of the sole trader are being considered.

Financing the Sole Trader and Partnership

The initial capital requirements of a sole trader or of a partnership are usually met by the introduction of cash or other assets by the owner or partners. This may be supplemented by loans from friends or members of the family, perhaps even on interest-free terms. (This, of course, is by far the best method of financing, if such generous relatives can be found.) Once the business has become established and achieved a good "credit rating", it will be able to meet short-term cash requirements from the bank either on overdraft or by a loan; and to some extent it will be able to finance its trading transactions on credit, e.g. by paying for last month's purchases from this month's sales.

Financing of Companies

The management accountant is most likely to be concerned with the financing of a business which operates as a limited company. The importance of limited liability is that the shareholders are liable only for any unpaid amounts on their shares and once these are fully paid, as the majority are, their liability ceases, regardless of the extent of the liabilities of the company in which they hold shares.

We will consider the financing of a company under the same three broad classifications used in Chapter 1, i.e. permanent, medium-term and short-term capital.

Permanent Capital

The principal method of obtaining permanent capital is by the issue of shares. The Companies Acts 1948 and 1967 do not specify the type of shares which a company must issue and such matters are covered in the Articles of Association, i.e. the internal rules of the individual company. The investors who will subscribe for the shares are mainly interested in the risk, the expected yield, and the voting powers of the shares, while the company issuing them will be attempting to obtain finance at the lowest cost.

The two main classes of shares are ordinary shares and preference shares.

Ordinary Shares. The majority of shares issued are ordinary shares. They have a nominal value, e.g. 5s. or £1, and they may be issued at a discount or at a premium. If issued at a discount they are subject to strict control under Section 57 of the Companies Act 1948. The ordinary shareholder provides the main risk-bearing capital of the business and as such he is entitled to a share of the surplus profits after the debenture holders and preference shareholders have been paid. As the ordinary shareholder receives only a share of the profits after the rights of the preference shareholder and debenture holder have been satisfied, it is only natural for him to expect to receive a bigger percentage of the profits then they receive. He is, after all, bearing the risks, and is the first to suffer if the level of profit drops. Because of the risk element ordinary shareholders may rightly expect to have some say in the way in which the business is run. This is achieved by attaching voting rights to the ordinary shares which allow the holders to vote at company meetings. In certain circumstances non-voting shares are issued, e.g. where it is wished to retain control in the hands of the original shareholders but where it is also necessary to obtain new capital. Such shares have been subject to a great deal of criticism over the past few years, and a number of companies have converted non-voting shares into voting shares as the opportunities arose.

Preference Shares. Preference shareholders are entitled to receive a fixed rate of dividend before any profits are divided among the other classes of shareholder. The shares are usually cumulative, i.e. if there are insufficient funds to pay the full rate of dividend in any particular year, that sum must be added to the dividend payment for the next year and the full payment must be made before other shareholders can participate in profits. If shareholders are given the right to a second dividend, e.g. 1% for every 5% paid to ordinary shareholders in excess of 10%, the shares are known as participating preference shares. A company may be authorised by its Articles to issue redeemable preference shares. These allow the company to obtain initial capital and later, when earnings increase, to redeem these shares and so enable a larger distribution to be made to the remaining shareholders. However, if the shares are redeemed out of profits there must be an equivalent amount transferred to a Capital Redemption Reserve Fund, in order to maintain the capital at its original figure and so protect the shareholders' interests. It should be noted that preference shares are rarely issued in a modern capitalisation.

Loan Capital—Long-term

Loan capital does not form part of the share capital and usually takes the form of a debenture. The debenture is the document which acknowledges the loan and also stipulates the terms and conditions upon which the loan is based; e.g. the rate of interest payable and the charge, if any, on the company's assets. If there is such a charge, the debenture holder is placed in the position of being a secured creditor ; if there is no charge he will be an ordinary unsecured creditor. These latter debentures are known as simple or naked debentures and because of the lack of security they can usually be issued only by firms with a high financial standing. They may carry the right to convert the nominal value of the debenture into ordinary shares at a future date and this can often prove an attractive proposition to an investor.

The more usual type of debenture is the mortgage debenture which gives a charge over the company's assets. The charge may be specific, e.g. on a building or plot of land, or—more usual—a floating charge may be given on the whole of the concern's assets. The main disadvantage with a fixed charge is that the concern is restricted in the way in which it can handle the charge; e.g. it cannot sell it. With a floating charge, however, assets may be dealt with in the normal way until such time as the concern defaults on a condition of the debenture, when all the assets as they then exist become the subject of a fixed charge. Any charge created by the concern must be registered with the Registrar of Companies within twenty-one days. The company may redeem debentures by buying them on the stock market before the actual date for redemption, otherwise the whole debenture issue becomes redeemable on the due date. There is frequently a period for redemption to take place. For example, a debenture dated 1970/75 means that redemption may take place any time between 1970 and 1975, usually at the option of the company, but redemption must be made by the 1975 date.

Medium-term Capital

The main sources of medium-term finance are bank loans, mortgages, sale and lease back of property, hire purchase and equipment leasing. These will now be considered in more detail.

Bank Loans. As a result of the recommendations of the Radcliffe Committee report published in 1959, banks are now willing to grant longer-term loans (i.e. for periods in excess of twelve months) to the small industrial and business units. The loans are usually made to enable the concern to improve or purchase capital assets, and the maximum figure will not normally exceed £10,000. The main benefit of these term loans, as they are called, is that there is no danger of the loan being prematurely recalled. This is always the problem facing the businessman who uses overdraft facilities and such recalls are often made when he can ill afford to make the repayment.

Mortgages. Mortgages which may be available to the business from such institutions as insurance companies, investment companies and trust funds are similar to debentures which have already been considered. The money borrowed forms a charge upon the assets of the company and if the business defaults on the mortgage interest repayments, the insurance company, etc., may take possession of the asset. The period of the mortgage will vary from approximately five to twenty years. This method of finance is usually an expensive one; high rates of interest have to be paid, and heavy conditions may be stipulated.

Sale and Lease Back of Property. If the business needs additional finance it may sell any valuable property which it owns to a property investment company under an agreement allowing the business to lease back the property from the investment company at an agreed rate, for a specified period with the option of renewal at the end of the original lease. This is a valuable method of obtaining a permanent increase in working capital, but it should be remembered that fixed rental charges will have to be met over a period of years when profits may fluctuate widely. There is also a reduction in the value of the fixed assets, but this will only occur to the extent of the difference between the value shown in the books prior to the sale and the value of the lease.

Hire Purchase. The main advantage of buying assets on hire purchase is that the business is able to use the earnings from employing the asset to pay the hire-purchase charges as they fall due. The asset must normally have a longer expected life than the length of the hire-purchase agreement, and the value should also be in excess of the amount outstanding on the agreement. This will mean that no extra security for the asset will be required.

The main disadvantage of hire-purchase financing is that the interest rates are usually fairly high, i.e. around 12% p.a. As this rate is applied to the full amount of the purchase price the *effective* rate of interest is nearly double the actual rate (i.e. in this instance 24% p.a.) which makes this method of financing very expensive. If an asset is purchased outright, then in addition to saving the hire-purchase charges all the earnings of that asset can be used for furthering the business's activities. Also the risk of obsolescence, although it exists the same no matter how the asset was financed, will be reduced to a greater degree since outright purchase means that payments will not still have to be made on an asset which has ceased to earn revenue for the business.

The main types of business using hire purchase as a means of finance are those whose work necessitates their expenses and profits being spread over a lengthy period, e.g. the building construction industry. Once the payments have been completed the ownership of the asset normally passes to the hirer, i.e. the business.

Credit Sale. Another form of purchase similar to hire purchase is known as credit sale. It is not subject to quite so many legal formalities as hire purchase and the ownership of the goods passes at the time of the agreement rather than remaining with the owner until the end of the agreement, as in hire purchase.

Equipment Leasing. This is very similar to leasing of property already considered. Although equipment leasing is a relatively new concept in Britain it has operated in America for many years. A finance company buys the equipment required by the business and then leases it to them on a contractual basis for a set period. This should not be confused with hire-purchase financing as there is never any question of the ownership passing to the business under a lease. Leasing is an obvious way for a business with limited capital resources to be able to expand its activities in the hope that the revenue earned from the leased equipment will more than repay the fairly high leasing charges. Leases on equipment will usually be

for about five years with the possibility of an extension at
a reduced rental, but much will depend on the type of
equipment to be leased. An everyday example of
equipment leasing is the renting of television sets by
individuals from firms specialising in this activity.

Financial Institutions

In addition to the methods already considered there are a
number of financial institutions which have been established to finance specific types of business or trade. The
main ones are:

- (a) The Finance Corporation for Industry Ltd.
- (b) The Industrial and Commercial Finance Corpora-
    tion Ltd.
- (c) The Ship Mortgage Finance Co. Ltd.
- (d) The Agricultural Mortgage Corporation Ltd.
- (e) The Exports Credit Guarantee Department.

I propose to outline the operation of the first two of these
institutions only, as they have the widest scope for giving
assistance to commercial and industrial concerns.

(a) *The Finance Corporation for Industry Ltd.* This
Corporation was established in 1945 and is itself financed
by the Bank of England and a number of investments
trusts and insurance companies. Loans are only available
for amounts of £200,000 and over and the intention is to
supplement rather than replace existing financial resources. The Corporation is willing to consider providing
medium-term capital to any industry without restrictions,
other than that the money will be used for expansion and
development within Britain. The main purpose of the
F.C.I. is to bridge the gap between short- and long-term
loans which other institutions are reluctant to fill. This
medium-term finance is usually too long for the banks and
too short for the individual insurance and investment
companies.

(b) *The Industrial and Commercial Finance Corporation
Ltd.* This Corporation was established with government
approval although not coming under its control. The
equity is held by the Bank of England and the Joint Stock

Banks and loans ranging from £5,000 to £300,000 are made to companies for the purpose of providing loan and additional share capital to enable the permanent asset structure to be more soundly based. The small company with sound management is most favoured, and repayments may be spread over varying periods up to twenty years if necessary. Also managed by the I.C.F.C. is the Estate Duties Investment Trust which is concerned with assisting private companies' shareholders to make provision for estate duty on their holdings, particularly where such holdings are a large proportion of total resources.

Industrial Holding Companies

A further method by which a company, particularly a small one, can obtain capital is to align itself with one of the industrial holding companies such as Norcross or The Thomas Tilling Group. What usually happens is that the takeover arrangements by the holding company provide for the existing management to stay on and run the company. The small company therefore acquires the facilities and resources of a large financial group without the need to sacrifice its independence completely. The holding company acts rather like an investment company spreading its business over a wide field and providing little interference with the management of the group members, but the small concern is no longer the same independent entity it was and may have to account for its actions to the holding company.

Short-term Capital

The main sources of short-term capital are bank overdraft, acceptance credits, delay in paying creditors and retained funds.

Bank Overdraft. This is probably the most commonly used method of obtaining short-term finance. The rate of interest is usually between 1 and 2% above Bank Rate with a minimum of 5%. A business would normally operate on an overdraft limit agreed with the local bank manager. This would mean that the business could go into overdraft at any time provided the limit was not exceeded. Interest is paid only on the outstanding daily balance, which makes it cheaper than obtaining a loan at a fixed rate of interest. The main drawback of overdrafts is that the borrower may be required to repay the amount outstanding at any time by the bank. Such demands are usually made during a period when credit is in short supply, which is the very time when the business needs to use its overdraft to the full.

Acceptance Credits. This method of finance is normally cheaper than bank borrowing, but the difference is usually only significant when dealing in large sums. The system operates as follows. The business will open an account with a merchant bank which specialises in acceptance credits. The bank will issue a letter of credit to the business, once it has established its financial standing, and the business may now draw bills of exchange which will be accepted by the accepting house, thereby making them "prime bank bills". These may be discounted, i.e. sold to a discounting house (the House paying a sum less than the full value of the bill which represents an interest payment). When the bill becomes payable, usually ninety days after it was drawn, the business will provide the accepting house with the necessary funds to meet it. It will however have had the use of that money, less a small amount paid to the discounting house as interest, for the period of the bill, i.e. ninety days.

Once this type of arrangement is in operation, it is generally possible to renew it for say another period of ninety days on the expiry of the current credit.

Delay in Paying Creditors. Although not an obvious source of capital it will be apparent that if the business is able to arrange with certain of its larger creditors to delay settlement of their accounts for a specific period it will be able to use the cash which would otherwise have been paid over to them. However, such arrangements are likely to be of a very temporary nature, and persistent requests for such facilities may result in the good credit rating of the business being downgraded.

Retained Funds. A major source of capital consists of funds which are retained in the business either in the form of profits not distributed to shareholders, or provisions and reserves set up for specific purposes (e.g. depreciation), or for general purposes (e.g. a general reserve fund).

Internal finance is the cheapest form of financing expansion, but it will be limited by the total amount of profit earned and the dividend policy which is followed by the individual business. It is now usual practice for the rate of dividend to be stabilised over a period so that it pays approximately the same rate of return each year on the capital contributed. If the capital increases the same rate of dividend would mean a higher proportion was required of the profits to pay for it; therefore increased earnings from employing the new capital must be at least equal to previous rate of earnings in order to finance the dividend without increasing the percentage required from profits.

Consider the following simplified example (ignoring taxation) :

Balance Sheet at End of Year 1

	£		£
Capital (8,000 £1 shares)	8,000	Assets	10,000
Profit	2,000		
	£10,000		£10,000

If the company's policy is to pay as a dividend 50% of its profits then each shareholder will receive 2s. 6d. for every share he owns.

$$\frac{\text{Profit available for distribution}}{\text{Capital}} \quad \frac{£2,000}{£8,000} \times 50\% = 2s.\ 6d.$$

If during Year 2 the share capital is increased to £10,000 and the profit remains the same, then the shareholders will now only receive 2s. per share.

$$\frac{\text{Profit available for distribution}}{\text{Capital}} \quad \frac{£2,000}{£10,000} \times 50\% = 2s.$$

For 2s. 6d. per share to be paid the distributed profit percentage must be increased to approximately 63%, leaving only 37% of the profit available for internal use within the company.

For the original percentages to apply and still result in all the shareholders receiving 2s. 6d. per share as a dividend the profit for the second year must be £2,500.

Thus

Profit available for distribution $\dfrac{£2,500}{£10,000} \times 50\% = 2s.\ 6d.$
Capital

The rate of increase in the capital is exactly the same as the rate of increase on earnings, i.e. capital increase from £8,000 to £10,000 represents 25% increase as does the increase in profit available, from £2,000 to £2,500.

Gearing

The amount which an ordinary shareholder is likely to receive by way of dividend is also governed by the gearing of the particular company. The term gearing is used to describe the ratio between the ordinary share capital section of the capital structure and the fixed interest capital. A highly-geared capital structure is one in which the fixed interest part forms a large part of the total, i.e. the ordinary shareholder is in a minority. A low-geared company is therefore one in which there is little fixed interest capital.

As you will remember, the ordinary shareholder receives a dividend only after all the fixed interest capital has been paid and obviously the more of this capital which has prior claim on profits the less chance the ordinary shareholder has of receiving anything, as he is last in the queue.

Let us consider two examples showing extreme high and low gearing.

Each company has a total capitalisation of £500,000. It is made up as follows:

	Company A	Company B
	£	£
Ordinary shares	400,000	100,000
Fixed { Preference shares (8%)	50,000	250,000
Debentures (10%)	50,000	150,000
	£500,000	£500,000

Gearing ratio = 4 : 1 $\dfrac{£400,000}{£100,000}$ $\dfrac{£100,000}{£400,000}$ 0·25 : 1

Company A is low geared (i.e. it has a high ratio) while Company B is highly geared (i.e. one with a low ratio).

It will be seen that the cost each year to Company A to enable it to finance its fixed capital is £9,000. This is made up of preference dividend £4,000 plus debenture interest, £5,000.

The cost to Company B is £35,000 made up of £20,000 on the preference shares and £15,000 on the debentures.

It should be noted that debenture interest is a charge against profits, before taxation, while dividends are an appropriation of profits after taxation.

It is clear from the above figures that profits available to ordinary shareholders are subject to a much greater degree of fluctuation in a highly-geared company than in a company with a low gearing.

Let us assume that the two companies had identical profits for two successive years, before charging debenture interest, these being £105,000 in the first year and £85,000 in the second. Taxation is assumed to be 50% and all the available profit is distributed.

Year 1

	Company A	*Company B*
	£	£
Profit before charging debenture interest	105,000	105,000
Debenture interest	5,000	15,000
	100,000	90,000
Taxation—50%	50,000	45,000
Profit available for distribution	50,000	45,000
Preference dividend	4,000	20,000
Profits distributed to ordinary shareholders	£46,000 (11·5%)	£25,000 (25%)

Year 2

	Company A	Company B
	£	£
Profit before charging deben- ture interest	85,000	85,000
Debenture interest	5,000	15,000
	80,000	70,000
Taxation—50%	40,000	35,000
Profit available for distribution	40,000	35,000
Preference dividend	4,000	20,000
Profits distributed to ordinary shareholders	£36,000 (9%)	£15,000 (15%)

The figures in parentheses represent the rate percentage on the ordinary share capital.

It will be seen that a reduction in profit of 19% from Year 1 to Year 2 has caused a fall of dividend rate in the case of Company A of 22%, i.e. from 11·5 to 9%; but in the case of Company B, because of the high proportion of the second year profit (i.e. £35,000) which has to be paid out to the fixed interest section of the capitalisation the dividend rate falls by 40% from 25 to 15%. This type of fluctuation is very disturbing for the ordinary share-holder in such a company.

Buying shares in a highly-geared company can there-fore be a hazardous experience, but of course just as a fall in profits produces a substantial reduction in the ordinary share dividend percentage, a rise in profits will cause a more than proportional rise in this dividend. Consider in our two companies that profits for Year 3 were £135,000.

The position now would be:

	Year 3	
	Company A	Company B
	£	£
Profit before charging debenture interest	135,000	135,000
Debenture interest	5,000	15,000
	130,000	120,000
Taxation—50%	65,000	60,000
Profit available for distribution	65,000	60,000
Preference dividend	4,000	20,000
Profits distributed to ordinary shareholders	£61,000 (15·3%)	£40,000 (40%)

If the dividend percentages for Years 2 and 3 are compared it will be seen that the increase in profit has resulted in a much more than aproportionate rise in the rate of dividend available to Company B ordinary shareholders.

The importance of gearing to the company and to the investor is likely to be somewhat different. The company will want to ensure as little interference as possible either now or in the future from preference shareholders and debenture holders, so the larger the proportion of ordinary shareholders the better.

There are two basic types of investor. One who is looking for a steady and regular income with prospects of long-term growth and the other who is willing to bear high risks in return for high dividends. In general the first type of investor will prefer a low-geared company and the second type a high-geared one. One further point to be considered is that a company which is already highly geared, particularly if the fixed interest capital takes the form of debentures, is likely to find difficulties in increasing its capital in the future, whereas the low-geared company can always have recourse to debentures if its expansion programme requires an influx of additional permanent capital.

Questions

1. What do you understand by the term "limited liability"?

2. Explain the main differences between ordinary shares and preference shares.

3. Outline the advantages and disadvantages of obtaining funds by the sale and lease back of property.

4. What is the main disadvantage of hire-purchase financing?

5. Outline the operations of the Industrial and Finance Corporation for Industry.

6. Explain why delay in paying creditors is a source of finance.

7. What do you understand by the term "capital gearing"?

8. If a company retains 50% of each year's earnings in the business and pays the remaining 50% to the shareholders would you expect to see profits rising each year?

9. A low-gearing ratio implies that a company is ...... geared and it has a large/small amount of fixed interest capital.

10. Should the investor who is seeking a steady and regular income invest in a high- or low-geared company?

Chapter 4

FUNDS FLOW ANALYSIS

It has already been pointed out that a business is a continuing entity and during the course of business operations many changes take place in assets, equities, income and expenses. The funds which are used in a business must be constantly on the move. There must be an even flow through the cycle of operations with no bottlenecks or dead ends. One of the best ways to illustrate the use of funds in the business is to liken them to the domestic hot-water system. The usual arrangement in the home is to have a cold-water storage tank into which the main injection of water flows. Once the system is established, i.e. when the storage tank is full, a continuous process is brought into operation. If you draw hot water from, say, the bathroom tap, as the level in the storage tank falls it is replaced from the mains until it is full once again. If for any reason the mains water is not available it will still be possible at first to draw water from the bathroom tap; but eventually the storage tank will be empty and the whole system will break down.

Let us now see how this continuous flow process operates in a business. Consider the diagram on page 35.

It will be seen that the initial injection of funds comes from the shareholders, and loan capital. Further injections may be made from time to time by short-term loans, e.g. bank overdraft. This initial injection of funds will be used to buy the necessary assets to enable the concern to begin operations; and in addition there must be sufficient funds to finance production until the results of such production are sold and the cash is received by the business.

Once the cash from sales is received (immediately in the case of cash sales, but perhaps not for a month or more when goods are invoiced to the customer) the continuous cycle begins. The receipts may be used to finance further

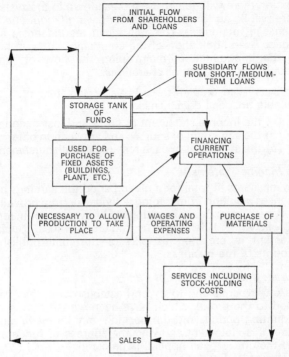

(The inflows from sales should exceed the outflows representing expenses. This excess (i.e. profit) will then result in further outflows covering taxation, dividend payments and the purchase of new assets etc.)

production which in turn will result in new sales. The sales should exceed the cost of producing the goods, the difference being profit, which is of course available for distribution to the shareholders but a proportion of which would be retained in the flow to allow for further expansion and development of products.

It will be seen that sales are vital if the process is to be a continuous one. As with the domestic hot-water system, if the main supply, in this case sales, is reduced or stops altogether there is likely to be little immediate effect on production, but, unless action is taken to remedy the situation there will quickly be a breakdown in the system. There will be no funds available for paying labour and for purchasing materials. This will mean redundancies and perhaps even liquidation of the company. You can now see the importance of maintaining the flow of funds through all the stages of operations.

It is usual to prepare three basic flow statements from available financial data. These are:

    (a) the income statement or profit and loss account;
    (b) the statement of sources and application of funds;
    (c) the statement of cash receipts and disbursements.

The Income Statement

This measures in total for a given period the earnings and expenses resulting from trading activities or from providing a service. An excess of earnings is known as net income or profit while a deficiency is known as a loss. Such a statement is prepared as part of the final published accounts of the business.

Sources and Application of Funds

It is often perplexing to try and establish what has happened to the profits which have been earned during the accounting period, and the position may be made much clearer if a statement showing the sources of funds and how they have been applied is prepared.

Sources of Funds:

    (a) profits, before charging depreciation;
    (b) new capital introduced during the period;
    (c) new long- or short-term loans;
    (d) reductions in short- or long-term assets, e.g. investments sold;
    (e) proceeds from the sale of fixed assets, e.g. sale of factory.

Application of Funds:

    (a) payment of dividends to shareholders;
    (b) reduction in long- or short-term liabilities;
    (c) increase in short- or long-term financial assets;
    (d) payments for the purchase of new fixed assets.

Item (*a*) in the sources statement perhaps deserves some explanation. Depreciation is a correct charge against the profits for the year as it is an attempt to place a monetary value on the extent to which an asset has been reduced in value during the accounting period. (More will be said about the problems of such valuations in a later chapter.) However, the charge for depreciation involves no actual outflow of funds; it is merely a book entry and it must therefore be added back to the net profit figure. The total sources of funds in any accounting period must equal the total application of these funds. An initial difference between the two sides of the statement will represent an increase or decrease in net working capital.

Net Working Capital

Before examining a practical problem involving source and application of funds let us consider what is meant by net working capital and why it is of such importance. Working capital is generally defined as the excess of current assets over current liabilities. This will include the following items under Current Assets:

> Stocks
> Debtors
> Cash at Bank
> Cash in Hand

and under Current Liabilities:

> Creditors (including current taxation)
> Bank Overdraft

It is from these items that the real "flow" of funds is generated. Stocks (raw materials) are needed to enable continuous production to take place and stocks (finished goods) to enable orders from customers to be met without delays. Debtors arise as a result of sales, and creditors as a result of purchases, both on credit terms. The bank and cash balances are needed to meet the delay in payment which occurs between the incurring of the expenses of production and the receipt of the revenue from sales. It is essential to try and convert both debtors and stock into cash as soon as possible, as only after such conversion can profits be realised. On the other hand, when the cash is received it should not be just left in the bank as it does not help the business to expand unless it is put to work either by increasing current operations, if there is sufficient demand for the concern's products, or by investing in fixed assets with an eye on future expansion, or in equities outside the business.

Working capital is therefore essentially circulating capital; but the desirable ratio between fixed and circulating capital will vary greatly, depending on the type of business. A shipbuilding firm, for instance, will require a large amount of fixed capital such as the shipyard and ancillary equipment; while the racecourse bookmaker will require very little fixed capital but a fairly large sum for working capital.

Management is concerned with two very important problems in which working capital plays a part. These are maintaining profitable operations and maintaining a solvent financial position. Profits are very important, but a firm must also be able to pay its debts when they fall due. It is possible for a firm to expand so rapidly that its whole financial solvency is brought into question because there is insufficient current circulating capital to pay for the expansion. This is known as over-trading, and has been the downfall of many apparently successful companies.

Each of the individual items which constitute working capital is capable of being controlled with a view to ensuring that the maximum amount of working capital is always available.

Stocks. Attention should be paid to stock levels, and minimum/maximum stock levels should be established. The cost of stock-holding is the loss which is incurred because the capital tied up in the stock cannot be used for financing other activities or even invested in equities, etc. The aim should be to keep stocks as low as possible consistent with being able to supply the demands of production. One of the best examples of raw material stock control is found in the motor-car industry, where the materials have hardly arrived as stocks before they are required for production. The time interval is frequently less than a week.

Debtors. A constant check should be maintained to ensure that debtors pay their accounts by the due date. Incentives might be offered to encourage them to pay early, e.g. $2\frac{1}{2}\%$ cash discount if paid within seven days. Too much pressure to pay may, however, have the effect of making the customer take his trade elsewhere.

Creditors. Accounts should not be paid before the due date but where discounts for prompt payment are offered they should usually be accepted because they represent a good return on the money paid.

Cash. This has already been considered, but the dangers of financing expansion by bank overdraft should be noted. As already mentioned overdrafts may be called in by the bank manager at very short notice and this could have serious consequences for a concern which is already short of liquid resources.

Let us now consider a practical example.

Expando Products Ltd.

Balance Sheet as at 31st December

	Year 1	Year 2		Year 1	Year 2
	£	£		£	£
Issued share capital	80,000	80,000	*Fixed Assets at net*		
General reserve	5,000	10,000	*book values*		
Profit and loss a/c.	10,500	14,000	Land and buildings	64,000	70,000
Debentures 9%	12,000	10,000	Plant and machinery	20,000	23,000
			Furniture and fittings	12,000	7,000
Current Liabilities			*Current Assets*		
Creditors	6,000	8,000	Stock	8,500	8,000
Current taxation	4,500	6,000	Debtors	14,000	17,000
Bank overdraft	500	—	Cash	—	3,000
	£118,500	£128,000		£118,500	£128,000

Depreciation in Year 2 was as follows:

Plant and machinery, £2,000
Furniture and fittings, £3,000

From the balance sheet we establish the movement in working capital and the statement of sources and application of funds for Year 2 as follows:

Working Capital Calculation

	Year 1	Year 2	±
	£	£	£
Current Assets			
Stock	8,500	8,000	−500
Debtors	14,000	17,000	+3,000
Cash	—	3,000	+3,000
	22,500	28,000	+5,500
Less			
Current Liabilities			
Creditors	6,000	8,000	+2,000
Current taxation	4,500	6,000	+1,500
Bank overdraft	500	—	−500
	11,000	14,000	+3,000
Net working capital	11,500	14,000	
Increase in working capital			+2,500

Sources and Application of Funds

		£
Sources		
Increase in general reserve		5,000
Increase in profit and loss account		3,500
Depreciation		
Plant and machinery	2,000	
Furniture and fittings	3,000	
		5,000
		13,500
Sale of furniture and fittings (a)		2,000
		£15,500
		£
Applications		
Purchase of land and buildings (b)		6,000
Purchase of plant and machinery		5,000
Redemption of debentures		2,000
		13,000
Net increase in sources, i.e. addition to working capital		£2,500

Notes

(*a*) Furniture and fittings for Year 1 stood at £12,000. The figure for Year 2 is £7,000 which has been reduced by £3,000 depreciation. Without this depreciation the figure would have been £10,000 which is £2,000 less than Year 1. This means that £2,000 of furniture and equipment must have been sold during Year 2 which is a source of funds and is shown in the statement.

(*b*) The £5,000 is calculated in a like manner. If there had been no depreciation in Year 2 the figure for Plant and Machinery would have been £25,000. This represents an increase of £5,000 over the Year 1 figure and this is the amount spent on new plant during Year 2.

Let us now examine another illustration to show the value of preparing these statements.

The following statements are prepared for the Growfast Co., covering a three-year period:

	£000s	£000s	£000s
Capital and Liabilities	*Year 1*	*Year 2*	*Year 3*
Shareholders (including retained profits)	720	780	870
Long-term debt	—	300	500
Current liabilities	260	300	340
	980	1,380	1,710

	£000s	£000s	£000s
	Year 1	*Year 2*	*Year 3*
Assets			
Fixed assets *less* depreciation	400	850	1,170
Current assets	580	530	540
	980	1,380	1,710

	£000s	£000s
Sources of Funds	*Year 2*	*Year 3*
Profits (after charging depreciation)	140	190
Depreciation	50	80
Increase in long-term debt	300	200
Total sources	490	470

Application

Dividends to shareholders	80	100
Purchase of new fixed assets	500	400
	——	——
	580	500
Net increase/decrease in working capital	−90	−30

In Year 1 the current assets were equal to almost 60% of the total assets and the owners were providing all the capital needs of the firm; but by the end of Year 3 this percentage was just over 30% and the large increase in fixed assets was being mainly financed by the increase in long-term debt. Although the business was profitable over the period it was impossible to finance the expansion from its operations. Net working capital decreased in both Year 2 and Year 3 when, in fact, it should have been increasing to support the increased activity. The company is therefore in a very vulnerable position; and it may find it difficult in the future to meet its obligations, as a result of overtrading.

The difficulties of the Growfast Company have been highlighted by the preparation of these fund flow statements. They enable the vital role of working capital to be clearly seen and they can show the way in which improvements in the working capital position can be made. Attention is also focused on what resources are available for the acquisition of assets and for the repayment of long-term debt.

Another use of the technique of working capital analysis is in the preparation of working capital forecasts as part of the overall planning and budgeting procedure. Management will then be in a better position to make decisions on future policies and investments.

Statement of Cash Receipts and Disbursements

This statement is narrower in concept than the sources and application of funds statement, as the latter is concerned with transactions which affect the net working capital while the former is only concerned with transactions that have a direct impact on cash.

Management needs to know how much cash will be available to pay creditors, interest on loans, income tax, dividends, etc. In some months there may be insufficient cash to meet these commitments, and it will then be necessary to arrange for a short-term loan, usually on overdraft from the bank. In months when the cash receipts exceed the cash payments, proper use should be made of the extra cash, e.g. by either paying off a short-term loan or by investing it for a suitable period. With careful planning it should be possible to ensure that there is always sufficient cash available to meet obligations, with the cash balance kept to a minimum.

Many businesses are of a seasonal nature, e.g. tent manufacturing, fruit farming and deck-chair hiring. It is essential for such trades to prepare an operating cash budget for the full trade cycle so that plans can be made for additional finance which may be needed in the off-peak months. Bank managers usually insist on seeing such budgets before they agree to grant overdraft facilities to cover the lean months, as they want to know the earliest time which the overdraft can be repaid, and also wish to make sure that there will be sufficient cash available during the cycle to pay off the sum borrowed.

It is usual to prepare such budgets for a period of twelve months to give an overall picture of the cash position, but more frequent statements will be required for control purposes. These may be even daily as, for example, in the case of a local authority, when it is extremely difficult to assess the amount of cash which will be received on any one day.

An outline of a cash budget is shown below:

Cash Budget Covering the Period January to December 19xx

	Jan.	Feb.	March	...	Dec.
Receipts					
Cash sales					
Cash received from debtors	___	___	___		___
Payments					
Cash purchases					
Payments to creditors					
Wages payments					
Payments relating to selling expenses					
Payments relating to distribution expenses					
Payments relating to administration expenses					
Payments in respect of capital transactions					
Other . . . detail	___	___	___		___

Cash surplus/deficiency

Let us consider how a cash budget might be prepared for a new company for the first six months of its operations.

The Newcomers Co. Ltd. was established on the 1st January with a subscribed capital of £50,000. It purchased in that month buildings for £20,000, plant and machinery for £8,000, furniture and fittings for £6,000, stock for £7,000.

The estimated sales for the six months were January £2,000, February £10,000, March £12,000 and £15,000 for April, May and June, and debtors were expected to settle their accounts at the end of the second month after the sale.

Purchases of merchandise for the period were estimated to be January £1,000, February £6,000, March £8,000, April £10,000 and £12,000 for May and June.

Creditors accounts were to be paid the month following the purchase.

Wages paid each month were estimated to be £1,000 and other expenses estimated to be £800 per month.

The cash budget would be as follows:

	Jan.	Feb.	March	April	May	June
	£	£	£	£	£	£
Receipts and Balances						
Shares	50,000					
Sales			2,000	10,000	12,000	15,000
Balance b/f		7,200	4,400			
Balance overdrawn c/f			1,400	1,200	1,000	
	£50,000	£7,200	£7,800	£11,200	£13,000	£15,000
Payments and Balances						
Buildings	20,000					
Plant and machinery	8,000					
Furniture and fittings	6,000					
Stock	7,000					
Purchases		1,000	6,000	8,000	10,000	12,000
Wages	1,000	1,000	1,000	1,000	1,000	1,000
General expenses	800	800	800	800	800	800
Balance in hand c/f	7,200	4,400				200
Balance b/f				1,400	1,200	1,000
	£50,000	£7,200	£7,800	£11,200	£13,000	£15,000

The actual cash balance position revealed from this budget is:

	In hand	Overdrawn
	Balance	
	£	£
January	7,200	
February	4,400	
March		1,400
April		1,200
May		1,000
June	200	

It will be seen that after the first two months the company will be short of cash, March producing the largest deficit of £1,400. It is therefore possible from the outset for the company to make arrangements to cover this cash short-age, and if this statement is submitted to the bank manager with a request for overdraft facilities for the three-month period, March, April and May, of around £1,500, the liquidity problems of the first six months of trading should be overcome. Only by planning in this manner is it possible for the overall cash position to be established. Once the initial budget has been prepared it can be amended if necessary; and suitable action can be taken as alterations to forecasts become necessary.

The preparation of plans and budgets is not restricted to just the cash position of a company. It is possible, and necessary, to plan and budget for the whole operation of the business, both financial and non-financial.

The subject of budgeting and budgetary control will be considered in the next chapter.

Questions

1. Illustrate by using a diagram how funds flow through a business.
2. State which three basic flow statements are usually prepared from available financial data.
3. Outline the main sources and applications of funds.
4. Define working capital and explain its importance.

5. Explain the controls which management should institute over the various elements of working capital, i.e. stock, debtors, cash and creditors.

6. Why is depreciation added back to the net profit figure?

7. What do you understand by the term "overtrading".

8. Explain the importance of preparing cash budgets.

9. How frequently should cash forecasts be prepared?

10. If there has been an increase in working capital from Year 1 to Year 2 does the sources of funds exceed the applications of funds on Year 2? Give reasons.

Chapter 5

BUDGETING AND BUDGETARY CONTROL

Referring again to the Institute of Cost and Works Accountants' terminology, a budget is defined as "a financial and/or quantitative statement, prepared and approved prior to a defined period of time, of the policy to be pursued during that period for the purpose of attaining a given objective". Budgetary control is defined as "the establishment of budgets relating the responsibilities of executives to the requirements of a policy, and the continuous comparison of actual with budgeted results either to secure by individual action the objective of that policy or to provide a basis for its revision". These definitions are very much concerned with planning, and planning as such must form an important function of management, covering all aspects of business activity. Both long-term projects and day-to-day operations need planning in accordance with future expectations. The plan which is prepared to show how resources will be required and used over a period is known as a *budget*, the act of preparing the plan is known as *budgeting* and the use of the plan to control activities is known as *budgetary control.*

In Chapter 2 we showed that it was possible for a balance sheet to be prepared for an ordinary individual in the same way as balance sheets are prepared for sole traders, partnerships and companies. Similarly everyone prepares and uses a budget of one sort or another. An individual will estimate what he is likely to earn in the coming months and plan his expenditure on food, rent, car expenses, etc. In order to be able to control his expenditure it is normally necessary for him to set limits on how much he will spend on individual items. The housewife will budget for an even shorter period, usually a week. As actual expenditure is incurred a comparison can be

made with the budgeted estimate and revisions undertaken, depending upon whether actual expenditure exceeds or is less than the estimate.

A business will prepare a budget for similar purposes;
but it will need to be more detailed so that control can be
exercised over all aspects of the enterprise.

Advantages of Budgets

Despite the obvious advantages there are still many
businesses which never use budgets. They claim that
budgeting is possible in some concerns but not in their
own, because they maintain that there are too many com-
plications and uncertainties to make it worth while.
However, once a concern is persuaded to adopt budgeting
it rapidly becomes convinced of its benefits and is sur-
prised that it was ever able to succeed before introducing
the system. Certainly it will usually be found that the
leading concerns in any industry are those which use
budgeting, together with other relevant techniques such
as standard costing and variance analysis, to the full. The
preparation of a budget is itself extremely beneficial as it
forces the person responsible for incurring expenses or
for generating income to plan for the future, and to
anticipate changes and make suitable adjustments. Too
frequently a business is run on a day-to-day basis without
any thought being given to the future. The proprietor is
likely to finish up by fulfilling Mr. Micawber's second,
gloomy, prediction—"Annual income twenty pounds,
annual expenditure nineteen nineteen six, result happiness.
Annual income twenty pounds, annual expenditure
twenty ought and sixpence, result misery." The objectives
and goals of the business are then lost, or take a back seat
to current pressures; but unless these goals are prominent
the whole organisation lacks direction, and results are
difficult to predict.

To prepare the overall or master budget it is necessary
for all sections of the business to co-operate and to be
aware of other section's limitations as well as their own.
To prepare the actual figures it is necessary to have a sound
system of recording information; this in itself facilitates
better control, as the information obtained from such

records can be used to compare performances with the budget and as a guide for future budgets.

The preparation and use of budgets also ensures that all members of the organisation are aware of the need to conserve business resources, and are aware that they may be called to account for expenses which they incur.

It is possible for inefficiencies to be revealed either during the budget preparation period or when comparisons of actual performances with estimates are made.

Control becomes centralised while individual managers become responsible for their particular activity. This planning and control should result in maximum profitability being achieved because the planned use of resources yields better results than haphazard use.

Requirements for Budgeting

For a budgeting system to be effective it is necessary to have a sound organisation structure. It is then possible to create budget centres within such a structure with clearly defined responsibilities. Departments may be budget centres or, if such departments are large, sub-groupings may be arranged, e.g. a number of similar machines or a particular process. Each centre will have a manager or centre head who will be responsible not only for the preparation of the budget information for his centre but also for the actual results as compared with the original estimates.

It is helpful to prepare a budget manual which sets out the responsibilities of all persons connected with the budgeting system and the procedure to be followed. Each person should know what the system is and what are its objectives. He should know the procedure to be followed when submitting relevant information, including deadline dates and the various codes which may be in use. Such a manual will often be in loose-leaf form so that amendments are easily made. Experiments are at present being conducted into the value of using network analysis in budget preparation. This technique involves scheduling the various stages involved in budgeting and then preparing a logical sequence diagram which enables control to be exercised over the time element in the preparation of each stage.

It is necessary to have someone responsible for budget preparation. In a small concern this may be the job of the accountant but in a large concern a budget committee is frequently established which exercises overall control over the budgeting procedures. Such a committee will usually be chaired by the chief executive officer and may well consist of all the heads of the various departments.

The accountant may act as budget officer, co-ordinating the committee's work in addition to preparing his own budgets such as cash budget, capital expenditure budget and administration budget.

The budgeting system can be shown diagrammatically as set out on the following page.

The time-span for budgeting will vary depending upon the uncertainties involved and the type of business. Long-range budgets are usually concerned with capital expenditure and may span five or more years. Short-term budgets, e.g. the cash budget, may only cover a week. Master budgets which consolidate an organisation's overall loans are usually prepared on an annual basis, mainly to fall in line with taxation/accounting requirements. For control purposes it is usual to subdivide the annual budget into a monthly- or four-weekly period budget. This does create problems of allocation as many expenses do not occur evenly throughout the year, but variances are spotted sooner and action may be taken to remedy deficiencies immediately the monthly comparisons have been made.

It is important that the individual carrying out a particular task should be consulted when the budget for that task is being prepared. It is probably a good idea to allow the individual to prepare his own budget which can then be incorporated in the general budget for the particular cost centre. The advantages of involving the individual in budget preparation are as follows:

1. The person doing the job is in the best position to make reliable estimates.
2. He will realise that his work matters and that he is a member of a team working towards a common objec-

THE BUDGET PROCEDURE

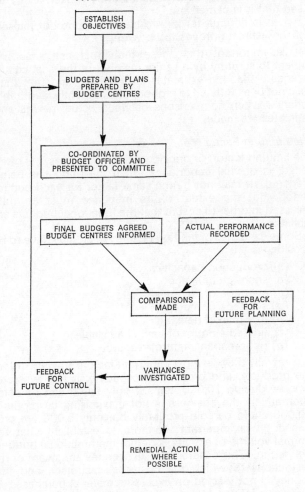

tive. He will also be able to appreciate how his section of work fits into the overall pattern.

3. If he makes his own estimate he is likely to try to see that it is carried out.

4. It is difficult for him to blame anyone but himself if the estimate proves to be wrong.

It is important that these individual estimates are subject to scrutiny by a senior member of the cost centre to ensure that the estimates are realistic, and that they have not been inflated to produce an apparently favourable variance when comparisons between actual results and estimates are made.

The Limiting Factor

The limiting factor, or principal budget factor as it is often called, is of vital importance when the budget is being prepared. It may not be the same factor for each budget period, but the extent of its influence must be fully assessed in order to ensure that the functional budgets are realistic.

Some examples of limiting factors which may have to be considered are:

(a) production capacity;
(b) shortage of space;
(c) shortage of key personnel;
(d) shortage of material;
(e) low market demand;
(f) limited amount of capital available;
(g) poor management of resources.

Generally the two most important factors are demand for the products, and production capacity. It is a waste of time producing 10,000 items if only 5,000 can be sold; alternatively the business is not maximising its profits if 10,000 could be sold profitably but only 5,000 are produced. It is important therefore to establish what the normal volume of activity is before the functional budgets are begun. This ensures that all sections are aware of the restrictions to which the business is subject, and that money is not wasted on excessive material purchases, or excessive labour costs, or "pie in the sky" budgeting.

Types of Budget

The Master Budget will comprise a number of Functional Budgets, i.e. those which relate to a particular function of the business, together with the Financial Budgets, i.e. the Cash Budget, the Statement of Sources and Application of Funds and the Budgeted Final Accounts. The main functional budgets are:

(*a*) Sales;
(*b*) Production;
(*c*) Plant utilisation;
(*d*) Manpower;
(*e*) Direct materials;
(*f*) Direct labour;
(*g*) Manufacturing overheads;
(*h*) Selling and distribution expenses;
(*i*) Administrative expenses;
(*j*) Cash;
(*k*) Capital;
(*l*) Financial.

All these budgets are, of course, interrelated: for example, it is not possible to draw up the materials purchase budget without knowing the type and quantity of product to be manufactured. A cash budget cannot be prepared until all the sales and expenses have been estimated.

It is usual, unless there are special circumstances, for a business to begin its budgeting by preparing the sales forecast for the budget period. This can then be used as a basis for the production budget, selling expenses budget, materials budget, cash budget, etc.

The relationship between the various budgets is shown diagrammatically on page 54.

As already mentioned the sales budget is usually of vital importance, but unfortunately it is also one of the most difficult to prepare. The sales budget will be based upon a sales forecast, which itself is subject to many factors, e.g. the pricing policy of the business, the general economic outlook and the outlook for the products of the particular business. For example, in times of austerity one might expect the sales of luxury goods to be reduced and the opposite to be the case in times of prosperity.

BUDGET RELATIONSHIPS

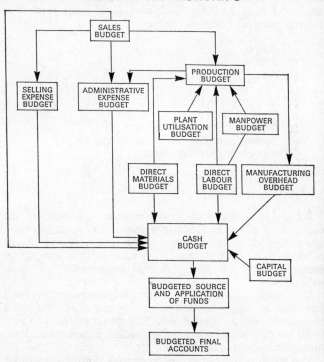

Sales Forecast

Much progress in this field has been made in recent years, but there is still a long way to go before the process is anywhere near perfect. The two main methods involve:

(a) opinion of salesmen and sales managers;
(b) market research and statistical techniques.

(*a*) *Opinion of Salesmen and Sales Managers.* As these are the people most directly concerned with sales their opinions can be a valuable guide to future sales. Each area sales manager and each salesman is issued with a forecast sheet for the coming period. Each individual prepares his own forecast, and these can then be compared and an overall sales estimate prepared. Only products which have been selling for some time should be included on the forecast sheet as it would be unfair to expect a salesman to estimate the demand for an entirely new product.

The usual information contained in such a forecast would be, for each product, the sales last year, average over a number of years, trend over say three years, and a column for the estimate.

This is illustrated as follows:

The Expando Co. Ltd.

Sales Forecast for the Year Ending 31st December 19xx

Sales Area..................
Salesman ....

Product	Average sales for last five years	Trend for past three years %±	Sales last year	Estimate
A				
B				
C				

(*b*) *Market Research and Statistical Techniques.* The purpose of market research is:

    (i) to determine the actual and potential field of sales;
    (ii) to study the methods to be used to create demand where it does not already exist, and to consider the adequacy of present methods of selling;
    (iii) to study the most effective means of distribution;
    (iv) to assess the potential purchasing power of the field of sales.

Data may be collected in a number of ways. It may involve consumer research, or perusal of trade journals and government publications such as the Monthly Digest of Statistics. The research may also be conducted by internal staff or by employing a specialist market research agency. The main information which market research should reveal is:

(i) where the customer buys goods of the class in question;
(ii) how frequently and in what quantities;
(iii) the effect of packaging on their decision;
(iv) the effect of price and "discounts";
(v) how they were led to choose one brand in preference to another.

Statistical Techniques

In connection with sales forecasting statistical techniques are basically the systematic collection and evaluation of data. Attempts are made to establish significant relationships; e.g. if there is an overall increase in the average wage this should result in a fractional increase in overall sales of certain products. If there is a forecast increase in the number of orders for steel products one would expect an increase in the demand for steel. Such correlations should be constantly sought as they often give an insight into the probable trend of sales.

It should be remembered that what has occurred in the past is no guarantee of what is likely to happen in the future. Even if market research is employed, the general trade situation and likely trends should always be considered. It is usual to employ most of these methods when compiling sales forecasts; but it should be remembered that external market research is expensive and it may be found that internal information is just as reliable and far cheaper.

Production Budget

The sales forecast becomes the sales budget, and this will be shown to the production manager to enable him to establish whether optimum use is being made of the facilities available. If there is insufficient productive capacity he is able to make alternative arrangements to ensure that demand is met.

These arrangements may be to:

(*a*) purchase new plant or hire the relevant equipment;
(*b*) introduce shift-working or increase overtime;
(*c*) sub-contract part of the production.

If the sales forecast does not need the production capacity the excess capacity must be scrapped, or new methods of increasing sales must be found. This may involve introducing discounts for bulk sales or more extensive advertising. (Market research will probably have revealed which would be the most profitable methods of advertising.) Spare machine time (e.g. a computer) may be hired out; but this will depend to a large extent on the type of machines which are not being fully used.

Manpower Budget

This involves forecasting the number of workpeople both direct and indirect who will be needed to meet the production requirements. In addition to the number of people required the various grades of labour will also be listed. This will allow the personnel department to plan the necessary recruitment; or to ensure that redundancies are kept to a minimum, if the work load is to be reduced, by arranging transfers if possible when vacancies occur. Training arrangements can also be planned to ensure the minimum disruption of production.

Plant Utilisation Budget

Schedules will be prepared to show the available load for each production department. By comparing these schedules with the production budget it will be possible to tell whether plant and machinery will be over- or underloaded. As with the production budget, if overloading is likely, alternative arrangements must be made; if underloading is the case, either the plant must be scrapped or sales increased to utilise the existing plant.

Materials Budget

This will show the raw materials and components which will be necessary to meet the production estimate, together with any finished materials purchased. It will be necessary to take account of opening and closing stocks and the current policy of management in connection with stock holding (e.g. whether stocks are to be run down or built up).

Cost of Labour Budget

Once the manpower budget has been prepared it will be possible to cost the various grades of labour and arrive at a labour cost budget.

Manufacturing Overhead Budget

This is a relatively difficult budget to prepare, as it is necessary to apportion the fixed overheads and the fixed portion of the semi-variable overheads to the various departments on some equitable basis usually related to production. More will be said about these expenses in the next chapter, but fixed and semi-fixed expenses are those which do not vary directly with production and which are incurred regardless of the volume of production; e.g. rent and rates or lease of buildings.

Selling Expenses Budget

The total costs incurred in selling and distributing the company's products will be ascertained and included in the selling expenses budget. The budget is connected with the total volume of sales but a number of expenses are not directly related to sales. Advertising will form part of this budget, but in some concerns advertising has come to play such an important part of the concern's activities that a separate advertising budget is prepared. Other expenses included in the selling expenses budget will be salesmen's salaries and commission, car expenses, sales office expenses and distribution expenses including warehousing costs and delivery costs.

The budget will normally be prepared by the sales manager after consulting the sales office manager, the advertising manager and the distribution manager.

Administrative Expense Budget

This budget is concerned with the cost of the administration section of the concern and will include such expenses as office salaries and upkeep, depreciation, stationery, managing directors' salary, telephones and postage. The accountant is usually responsible for preparing this budget.

Cash Budget

This has already been considered in the last chapter, but it is clear from the diagram on page 54 that nearly all the other budgets influence the cash budget, and it is usually one of the last budgets to be prepared.

Capital Expenditure Budget

This budget may have a different time-span from the other budgets: indeed it should be for a much longer period if planning is to be a major concern of management. The budget will show the future expenditure on fixed assets over a period of, say, five years, broken down into perhaps yearly sections. Different emphasis might be placed on different years; e.g. years four and five may only be tentative proposals. This budget is normally subject to strict top management control as large amounts of expenditure are usually involved.

The information to prepare the capital expenditure budget will come from:

(a) the plant utilisation budget, especially if this shows overloading;

(b) requests for new types of plant and equipment;

(c) requests for new vehicles;

(d) requests for new office machinery (e.g. a computer);

(e) the main development plans of the business, which will detail the new assets which are to be purchased in order to fulfil the planned expansion (e.g. new factory to be built).

The Master Budget

Once all the subsidiary budgets have been prepared it is possible to combine them into the master budget, which takes the form of a budgeted profit and loss account. It will be submitted to the budget committee together with the subsidiary budgets (which will already have been considered in detail) ; and if the committee approve it it will be forwarded to the board of directors.

A specimen master budget is shown below.

The Expando Co. Ltd.
Master Budget for the Year Ending 31st December 19xx
Budget based on ....% of Capacity

	Actual last year	Item		Adjusted budget for current year	Budget for 19xx
	£			£	£
1.		Sales			
2.		Cost of goods sold			
			Direct labour		
			Direct materials		
		Plus	Opening stock		
		Less	Closing stock		
			Manufacturing overheads		
			Total		
3.		Gross profit (1 *less* 2)			
4.		Selling and distribution expenses			
5.		Administrative expenses			
6.		Net profit (3 *less* 4 + 5)			
7.		Transfers to reserve funds			
8.		Dividends			
9.		Provision for taxation			
10.		Total appropriations			
11		Profit and loss balance carried forward to balance sheet (6 *less* 10)			

This master budget would be supported by a budgeted balance sheet, together with a budgeted statement of the sources and application of funds.

Flexible Budgetary Control

The type of budgets so far considered are known as fixed budgets; i.e. the budgets are based on one level of output and sales have been equated with production, etc. If this level of output varies from the estimate, there will be large variances, most of which should be taken care of by a "level of activity variance", but control does become difficult. Flexible budgetary control is designed to amend the budget figures as the level of activity changes. Many types of business have great difficulty in estimating sales with any accuracy because of external uncontrollable influences. For example, the plastic mackintosh industry is likely to have poor sales in a very dry summer, when conversely the soft drinks industry is likely to have bumper sales.

A flexible budget may be prepared for varying levels of output 60%, 70%, etc., up to 100%. The main requirement is that expenses should be analysed into three distinct categories:

(a) fixed expense, i.e. an expense which tends to be unaffected by variations in the volume of output;

(b) semi-variable expense, i.e. an expense which is partly fixed and partly variable;

(c) variable expense, i.e. an expense which tends to vary directly with variations in the volume of output.

Once this analysis is complete it is possible to prepare the different budgets for different levels of activity, which allows a greater degree of control to be exercised when the actual results are compared with the estimates.

Control

The preparation and approval of the master budget by top management is not the end of the budgetary process but merely the beginning. The whole purpose of budgeting is to establish standards with which actual performances can be compared. The budget officer should prepare a report at least once a month, showing how the actual expenses and income compare with the estimates. The principle of management by exception comes into force here. Once plans have been established, management is not really interested in the fact that they are working out as expected, since this was, after all, the original intention. They are, however, interested when the plans do not work out as expected. Their role in the organisation is to take appropriate action in such cases.

The monthly budget report should therefore emphasise the main variations from the planned figures; and explanations for such variances will be required from the person responsible for incurring them. The report should also be presented promptly. Speed is probably more important than absolute accuracy as the longer a variance is left the more difficult it becomes to isolate and remedy.

It should always be remembered that the whole budgetary system is based on estimates—estimated sales, estimated expenses, etc. The mechanical process of bringing the data together can be carried out exactly, but the final master budget is only as good as the estimates from which it was prepared. It may well be that a variation is due to bad estimating originally and this explanation should always be considered before recriminations are made.

Although budgetary control is an invaluable exercise, since it forces management to plan for the future and it establishes responsibility for all expenses and revenues, it is costly to operate. This factor must influence the extent to which a business commits itself to budgetary control. It is also of a short-term nature; i.e. it usually involves a twelve-month cycle enabling management to control current operations. Concentration on this annual cycle has the danger that strategic long-range planning may be neglected, and this could have adverse results in the future. The more progressive organisation may be using the budget to control costs for longer periods than twelve months by utilising rolling budgets, programmed budgeting, etc., particularly as a means of controlling capital expenditure. A rolling budget may cover a period of say, three years. At the end of the first year a further year is added to the two years remaining in the original budget period, thereby bringing the overall budget period back to three years. For example, if the budget covered the years 1971, 1972 and 1973, at the end of 1971 the budget for 1974 would be prepared and at the end of 1972 the budget for 1975 and so on. However, there are many more organisations who have not yet come round to installing simple budgetary procedures despite their apparent benefits.

Budgetary control should be just one of the techniques used by management in planning the overall strategy of control and development of the business.

Questions

1. Define "a budget", "budgetary control" and "budgeting".

2. Enumerate the advantages of preparing and using budgets.

3. Illustrate by means of a diagram the budget procedure.

4. Give some examples of limiting factors which may have to be considered when preparing budgets.

5. What are the two main methods of preparing a sales forecast?

6. What is the purpose of preparing a manpower budget?

7. Prepare a master budget in outline for some organisation with which you are familiar.

8. What do you understand by the term "flexible budgetary control"? What are the advantages of using such a system?

9. "The final master budget is only as good as the estimates from which it was prepared". Comment on this statement.

10. What are the dangers of too much attention being placed on the short-term budget?

Chapter 6

COSTING: I—HISTORICAL COSTING

In financial accounting, transactions are classified according to type and then summarised, to enable the annual financial statements and reports for shareholders to be prepared. The limitations of financial accounting as an aid to management were shown in the example in Chapter 1, pages 4 and 5.

Management requires much more detail than is available from the financial accounts if it is to run the business effectively. It will need to know how much it costs to operate a particular section of the business, or how much it costs to produce and sell a specific product or group of products. This detailed information is produced by the cost accountant, but it must not be assumed that cost accountancy is an entirely different accounting system. It is really only an extension of the general accounting system, a different interpretation being placed on costs by the cost accountant.

In financial accounting the costs are reported in aggregate while in cost accounting the costs are broken down under certain categories and charged to a cost centre on a unit basis. This recording of the actual costs is known as historical costing, and as such, it forms an essential part of any costing system. However, these costs do relate to past events and as such are no real aid to measuring efficiency. This can best be achieved by first establishing standards by which the actual costs can be compared, and then calculating variances and finding explanations for them. This is known as standard costing and will be dealt with in the next chapter.

Elements of Cost

The prime cost of a product consists of three basic elements:

(a) direct materials;
(b) direct labour;
(c) direct expenses;

These together form what is known as prime cost and all expenses over and above prime cost are known as overhead expenses.

Let us take a closer look at these three basic elements. They represent the only costs which can easily be directly allocated to a specific manufacturing cost centre. Overhead expenses are usually apportioned on some equitable basis to the individual cost centres, as they cannot be directly allocated.

Direct Material. This includes all materials relating to the specific job or batch whether drawn from stores or specially (separately) purchased. The information will be obtained from the stores requisitions and material invoices, priced at the appropriate rate for the amount of material used.

Direct Labour. This is the cost of labour which is directly traceable to the creation of the product. The labour may be skilled or unskilled; and the information is obtained from employees' time sheets or job cards, which have been completed by them and then processed by the wages department to reveal the cost in wages of each job appearing on a time sheet.

Direct Expenses. This represents any other direct costs which are incurred specifically for the particular job; e.g. royalties on production, carriage inwards, costs of special tests, and hire of special equipment. This information will be obtained from receipted accounts and invoices.

Overhead Expenses. The same material, labour and expense classification is used for overhead expenses but they are now called:

(a) indirect material;
(b) indirect labour;
(c) indirect expenses.

In general terms, "overhead" represents all the expenses which are not direct expenses, and are incurred in connection with the general organisation of the whole business. These expenses are subdivided into four main categories, namely:

    (*a*) production expenses;
    (*b*) selling expenses;
    (*c*) distribution expenses;
    (*d*) administration expenses.

The build-up of costs can be illustrated by the following diagram:

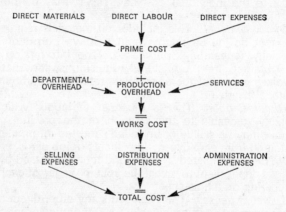

Production overhead includes all indirect expenditure incurred by the works from the receipt of the production order until the finished product is ready for despatch. Examples of expenses coming within this category are indirect materials (grease, cotton waste) indirect wages (foremen, cleaners) and general departmental expenses such as rent, lighting and heating of the factory. Services which are included in the production overhead will cover such sections as repair and maintenance, production control, etc.

Selling expenses include the cost of obtaining the orders for the goods; e.g. salaries and expenses of salesmen, advertising and sales showroom costs.

Distribution expenses cover all expenditure incurred in handling the finished product from the time of its despatch until it reaches its final destination. Examples are the upkeep and maintenance of delivery vehicles, warehouse costs and packing expenses.

Administration expenses are those which are incurred in controlling and directing the business, including offices, salaries and upkeep, depreciation of office machinery and directors expenses.

These overhead expenses are often referred to as "period costs" indicating that they are more related to time than to volume of production.

It will be appreciated that these overhead expenses form a large proportion of the overall expenditure of the concern; and it is a major problem to allocate these expenses to the individual products or jobs. It is usual to charge each job with a share of each works department through which it passes; and then to this total works cost an appropriate charge in respect of the other major overhead expenses, i.e. selling, distribution and administration is added.

Allocation of Production Overhead

The methods commonly adopted for allocation of production overhead are:

   (a) percentage on direct materials;
   (b) percentage on direct wages;
   (c) percentage on prime cost;
   (d) direct labour—hour rate;
   (e) machine hour rate.

The particular method adopted will depend on the type of production; e.g. where machines are the predominant factor in the manufacturing process, the machine hour rate will be most suitable. If time is the predominating factor, the direct labour hour has advantages.

It should be remembered that whichever method is adopted the resultant charge is only an estimate. There will rarely be complete agreement between the total charges made during a period and the actual overhead expenditure incurred during the same period. This is because it is necessary to estimate the overheads for the coming period and base the recharges on the budgeted figures. It would not be possible to decide upon a recharge figure for each job as it was completed if this were not done.

Let us consider an example of how a works overhead might be calculated for a particular job using the percentage of prime cost method.

	£
Estimated total works overhead for period	20,000
Estimated total direct materials for period	4,500
Estimated total direct labour for period	3,500
Estimated total direct expenses for period	500

Estimated overhead recovery rate

$$= \frac{20,000}{4,500 + 3,500 + 500} \times 100 = 250\%$$

This rate of 250% will now be applied to the prime cost of each individual job.

Say that job 123 is charged with the following direct costs:

	£
Direct labour	250
Direct material	200
Direct expenses	50
	──
Prime cost	500
Add works overhead at 250%	1,250
	──
Total works cost	£1,750

If the job has to go through a number of different cost centres then overhead cost rates (i.e. production overhead absorption rates) will be calculated for each cost centre, rather than a global figure as was done in the simple illustration above.

Where such separate cost centres are in operation the estimation of the overheads applicable to each cost centre must first be decided.

The object is to ensure that allocation of expenses reflects the facts as accurately as is possible when an arbitrary apportionment has to be used. An actual basis is the ideal to be used wherever possible ; e.g. depreciation of each machine can be allocated directly to the relevant centre. Where it is necessary to make some form of equitable allocation attention should still be directed to relevant activities ; e.g. rent and rates can be allocated on the floor space occupied by the cost centre, and canteen and welfare facilities in accordance with the number of employees working in each centre.

Recovery rates should be frequently reviewed as over- or under-recovery will tend to mean that selling prices, if based on total costs, are too low or too high.

Allocation of Selling and Distribution Expenses

There is frequently no relationship whatsoever between the amount of selling effort and the actual sale achieved. A telephone call may bring in a large order while a number of personal visits to a customer may result in a small order or even no order at all. However, if more than one product is sold it is essential, for accurate results to be obtained, that some agreed basis is adopted for allocation of selling expenses. This may take the form of a percentage on selling price or a rate per article sold. Special expenses incurred on one particular product should be charged to that product ; e.g. extensive advertising to launch a new item should not be recharged over all the products generally but to the new item. In this way it is possible to establish the real cost of each product. If the business produces only one type of product, selling and distribution expenses may be conveniently recharged as a percentage of works cost. Distribution expenses are often peculiar to a particular job or product and it should therefore be possible to calculate a fairly accurate rate per article distributed or rates per job to recover these expenses.

Allocation of Administration Expenses

These expenses are usually much smaller in amount than works expenses and are not closely related to production. However, as more sophisticated control techniques are brought into operation including the computer, this expense is becoming more important year by year.

The usual basis has been to allocate as a percentage on works cost, but more direct allocations may be necessary where it is possible to tie costs down to individual jobs. For example, computer time may be recharged on an hourly basis to cost centres within the overall administration expenses and to specific jobs if possible.

Reliability of Costing

Objections are often raised, particularly by the small concern, to the introduction of a costing system on the grounds of expense and this point should always be borne in mind. It is no use for a business which previously made a £100 profit to introduce a costing system only to find that because of the extra expense it incurs it now suffers a £100 loss. It is little satisfaction to the owners to be able to be shown how the loss arose.

Once established it is possible to place too much reliance on the costing system. A works manager might be asked to state the components of job 123 by his managing director and he would be able to reply quite accurately. But if the question was how much job 123 costs, his reply would of necessity be based on a number of estimates which would prevent absolute accuracy. It is essential that the person asking the questions should not expect as much accuracy in the answer to the second question as he might be able to in the first answer.

It is equally important to realise that just because a profit is made on each job in terms of the cost accounts it does not mean that the financial profit and loss account will reveal a similar healthy state. Certain items are omitted from cost accounts, e.g. loan interest, taxation and exceptional costs caused by, say, a fire. As these first two are originally management decisions management should be aware of them when determining profit margins; but a more difficult problem is the over- or under-recovery of overheads. It has already been pointed out that the recovery rate is based on estimated expenses and if the estimates vary from the actual then there will be over- or under-recovery. Both these states can give rise to inaccurate costing statements. Under-recovery of overheads will mean that the costed profit is too great, e.g.:

Estimated overhead   £5,000
Estimated machine hours   1,000
Overhead recovery rate   £5 per machine hour
Actual overhead   £4,000
Actual machine hours   700

The total amount recovered will be 700 × £5 = £3,500, but the actual overhead amounted to £4,000. This means that the costing profit is overstated by £500.

Over-recovery is equally as dangerous, as the pricing policy of the concern may be needlessly high and un-competitive because too high a charge is being made for overheads.

It is essential that reconciliation statements should be prepared at frequent intervals to ensure that after making the appropriate adjustments, the financial and cost ac-counts are in unison. The ideal situation is to have a fully integrated financial and costing system as part of the overall planning strategy using standard costing and budgetary control.

Costing Methods

Although the basic elements of costing apply to all con-cerns including non-profit-making bodies such as local authorities, hospitals, etc., the needs of various types of concern are different, and costing systems have been de-signed to suit particular types of organisation.

The three main types of costing systems are:

(a) job, contract or batch costing;
(b) process costing or unit costing;
(c) operating costing.

The first grouping is used where definite contracts or jobs are undertaken. Each job or contract is given a dis-tinct reference number to which all the direct costs are charged. Indirect costs will form only a small proportion of the total cost of the job, particularly in contract costing. Batch costing is an extension of job costing where there are a number of similar items to be manufactured, but it is still possible to identify the particular batch and reference it accordingly.

Concerns likely to use contract costing are public works contractors and shipbuilders. Heavy engineering works might use job costing for, say, the production of individual electric alternators; and this system would also be used by the jobbing builder, plumber, electrician, etc. Batch costing might be used to control the production of gear units or electric motors where perhaps a few thousand of each design are required.

A specimen Job Cost Sheet is shown below:

JOB COST SHEET

Works Order No.............

Particulars:.........................

....

DATE

CUSTOMER/DEPARTMENT:............ Commenced........ Completed........

DATE	REF.	DETAILS	DIRECT COSTS			WORKS
			Material £ s. d.	Labour £ s. d.	Expense £ s. d.	Overhead £ s. d.
			——	——	——	——
			═══	═══	═══	═══

Summary

Direct material
   „   wages
   „   expenses
Works overhead
            ——

ADD

Administration overhead
Selling and distribution
  overhead
            ——

Total cost
Profit   % on total cost ....
            ——
Selling price   Sales invoice reference..........
            ——

Process costing is applicable to concerns in which the product passes through a number of processes during its manufacture and it is required to ascertain the cost of each stage of the processing.

Such industries as soap-making, paper-making and distillation processes are all suitable for using this system.

The normal requirements for the system to operate effectively are that the end-product of one process should form the raw material of the next process, with any by-products of each process being accounted for in the process in which they occur. Examples of by-products are coke and tar in gas production, or cattle food in oil refining from copra.

A separate cost account is kept for each process, the allocation of costs being on the normal method already outlined. At the end of each period a cost sheet will be prepared to show the total and unit costs of each process, and for the finished product.

Unit costing or output costing is used where only one commodity is produced and it is not normally necessary to require an extensive analysis of costs. This system may be used by a brickworks, ascertaining the cost per 1,000 bricks, or a cement works ascertaining the cost per ton of cement produced. The cost sheet would show the costs incurred at each stage of manufacture under appropriate expense headings and the cost per unit of output during the period.

An example of a Process Cost Sheet is shown on the following page.

Operating Costing

This system is applicable to undertakings which perform a service rather than manufacture articles. The system is designed to show the cost of the service together with a cost per unit. Such services as hospitals (unit per patient/week) and police service (unit cost per 1,000 population served or per police officer) are examples. In many cases it is not necessary to keep a separate set of cost accounts as the financial accounts can be designed to produce the necessary figures for the unit calculations.

Of necessity this chapter gives only the briefest outline of historical costing, and it is intended to act primarily as an introduction to cost terminology which will be met in later chapters.

Historical costs may be useful for analysing past results and revealing weaknesses, but mistakes are not

PROCESS COST SHEET

Accounting Period:..............................

Item	Process No. 1 *Description* .... *Units Produced*			Process No. 2 *Description* .... *Units Produced*		
	Quantity	Value	Cost per Unit	Quantity	Value	Cost per Unit
Material in Process 1/x/xx						
Raw material						
Less material in Process 31/x/xx						
Process expenses (from Cost Accounts)						
Less value of residuals						
Loss in weight (a)	Nil	Nil		Nil	Nil	
Net works cost						
Corresponding figures last period						

(a) Loss in weight occurs in many processes and affects the quantity but not of course the cost i.e. there is no value attributed to the loss.

discovered or remedied until after the event. There is also no yardstick by which the actual results can be measured and it is insufficient to be satisfied with the fact that a profit has been made. Management needs to know whether profits are being maximised and assured that inefficiencies and wastage have been eliminated.

In order that management can control costs much more effectively and have something to measure results against it is necessary to operate a standard costing system.

The management accountant will be primarily concerned with the operation and results of such a system, and the next chapter will therefore be an attempt to outline the setting up and operation of a standard costing system.

Questions

1. What are the three basic costs which together form prime cost?
2. What do you understand by the term "overhead expense"?
3. Show by means of a diagram the build up of costs.
4. Enumerate the main methods of allocating production overhead to individual jobs.
5. Explain what is meant by the term "cost centre".
6. What are the dangers of under- or over-recovery of overheads?
7. Draw up a cost sheet suitable for job costing.
8. Which industries are most likely to use process costing?
9. What do you understand by the term "operating costing"? Outline the types of organisation most likely to use such a system.
10. Outline the usual methods of allocating administration, selling and distribution expenses to individual jobs.

Chapter 7

COSTING: II—STANDARD COSTING

The setting of standards as a basis of measurement and comparison applies to many different fields of activity. A school, for example, will establish standards by which academic achievements may be measured and compared, or an inspection department in a manufacturing plant will set standards against which actual production can be measured and either be passed or rejected.

A standard may therefore be said to be a basis for the measurement of the adequacy or inadequacy of the results from a particular activity. When applied to cost accounting, standard costing involves the establishment of pre-determined costs usually on a unit basis; i.e. a standard quantity of materials, a standard labour rate, a standard time and a standard overhead rate, necessary to produce a given unit of output. The standards will remain unchanged as long as the method of operation and basic prices used to set the standards remain the same.

The differences between the actual costs and the standard costs are known as variances, and the breakdown of the total variances into different components is known as variance analysis.

The main advantages of standard costing are:

1. The setting of standards involves establishing the most efficient methods of producing the unit which in itself may lead to economies.

2. Actual performance may be compared with a pre-determined standard revealing favourable or adverse variances and also allowing the principle of "management by exception" to operate when everything is going according to plan.

3. Cost consciousness is stimulated throughout the organisation.

4. It is possible to establish which variances are due to external influences (e.g. a price increase over which management have little control) and which are caused by internal influences.

5. By the establishment of cost centres it is possible to define responsibilities. (A cost centre may be a location, a person or an item of equipment to which costs can be allocated and used for control purposes.)

Budgetary control and standard costing are closely linked as they both involve the forecasting of expenses and the comparison of the actual results with the forecast. Although it is possible to operate one without the other it is usually much more satisfactory if they are operated together. For example, once standard costs are established it is easy to prepare the production and sales budgets, and the setting of the standard costs is made easier if a budget is already in existence which shows expected levels of output.

The word "standard" is meaningless unless it is qualified by a description of the type of standard being contemplated. Standards fall into three broad categories:

(*a*) strict or ideal;
(*b*) attainable or expected actual;
(*c*) loose.

Strict Standards

These represent the maximum of efficiency of all the cost elements and may be said to be the standard of perfection, which is obviously unrealistic and would only be experienced for very short periods of time. The setting of such standards may motivate employees to increase their output to the maximum, but if the standards are still not attained, their morale may be seriously affected.

Attainable Standards

These are the standards which are expected to be achieved in the period, with reasonable effort. The variations which do arise are more likely to be measures of superior or inferior performance rather than variances due to poor original standards. But it still may be that the standards are too low for the better type of employee and too high for the less skilled worker.

Loose Standards

If standards are easily achieved, actual results may be better than standard, allowing management to indulge in self-congratulation. However, such achievements may result in employees reducing their output to conform with the standards and there is certainly no inducement to increase their performance.

It is most beneficial if both an ideal and an expected actual standard are calculated. This ensures that actual results can be compared with two standards and prevents the expected standard from becoming a loose standard.

If standards are set which are expected to be in operation for some considerable time, they are called basic standards and when revisions become necessary they are made using index numbers. This is the same principle as that used to record the changes in the cost of living; i.e. a base period is fixed (say, 1st January 19xx = 100) and subsequent increases or decreases in the cost of living are represented by additions or subtractions to the basic 100 figure.

It is necessary to establish standards for each type of cost, i.e. labour, materials, overheads, and this will normally be the responsibility of the cost accountant. He must, however, work in close co-operation with other departments, and particularly with the time-and-motion study engineers whose work will have a great influence on the times set for the particular tasks.

Variances

One of the most valuable uses of standard costing as an aid to control by management is in the presentation of variances. Where actual results are better than the standard a favourable variance will be shown. When the results are worse than estimated an adverse variance arises.

Basically there are two types of variances: one results from a change in price and the other from a change in quantity or volume.

Several different variances are used to reflect particular reasons for differences occurring but they all depend on these two basic functions, price and quantity. The importance of variance analysis is as a controlling device, enabling management to ascertain the reason for variances from the people responsible for incurring them, and to take corrective action whenever necessary. It must be appreciated that every adverse variance has the effect of reducing the budgeted profit and the sooner action is taken to remedy such trends the less will be the effect on the final profit target.

The principal variances which we will consider are:

    (*a*) total cost variance;
    (*b*) direct materials cost variance;
    (*c*) direct wages variance;
    (*d*) overhead variance.

Different variances will be used by different industries but these four will be common to all. It will probably be appreciated that variance (1) is made up of variances (2) + (3) + (4). Each of these latter three variances is subject to further analysis to enable the effect of our two basic functions to be ascertained, i.e. price and quantity.

The diagram on the page 81 shows the relationships between the different types of variances.

It is important to remember that the difference between the actual cost and the standard cost of a particular activity is the total cost variance and each of the other variances must add up to this figure. Similarly the direct wages variance is a combination of the direct wages rate variance and the direct labour efficiency variance. It follows that if you have two out of three of these variances the other can be found either by subtraction or addition, i.e.:

Direct wages rate variance + Direct labour efficiency variance = Direct wage variance

or

Direct wages variance − Direct wages rate variance = Direct labour efficiency variance

However, it is as well to calculate all the variances to ensure that no errors have been made. It should be noted that the formula used to calculate the variances in this chapter are so framed that a positive result will mean a favourable variance and a negative result an adverse variance. This procedure differs from a number of textbooks, but it is felt that by adopting this system a better understanding of the concept of variance analysis is possible.

Material Cost Variance

This is the difference between the standard cost of materials specified for a particular operation and the actual cost of the materials used.

The formula is:

$$SC - AC$$
(Standard cost) − (Actual cost)

Material Price Variance. This is the difference between the standard price of the material specified and the actual price paid.

The formula is:

$$AQ (SP - AP)$$
(Actual quantity (Standard price − Actual price))

Material Usage Variance. This is the difference between the standard quantity which should have been consumed and the actual quantity used, calculated at the standard price.

The formula is:

$$SP (SQ - AQ)$$
(Standard price (Standard quantity − Actual quantity))

Let us consider a practical example:

It is estimated that 1 lb. of material will produce 10 articles. The standard price of material is £0·5 per pound. During a specified period 100 lb. of material were issued which cost £45 and the actual production was 1,100 articles.

COST VARIANCE ANALYSIS CHART

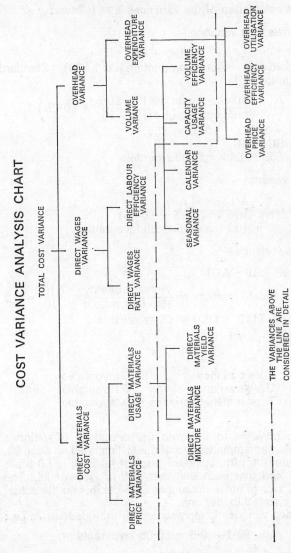

TOTAL COST VARIANCE

DIRECT MATERIALS COST VARIANCE

DIRECT WAGES VARIANCE

OVERHEAD VARIANCE

DIRECT MATERIALS PRICE VARIANCE

DIRECT MATERIALS USAGE VARIANCE

DIRECT WAGES RATE VARIANCE

DIRECT LABOUR EFFICIENCY VARIANCE

VOLUME VARIANCE

OVERHEAD EXPENDITURE VARIANCE

DIRECT MATERIALS MIXTURE VARIANCE

DIRECT MATERIALS YIELD VARIANCE

SEASONAL VARIANCE

CALENDAR VARIANCE

CAPACITY USAGE VARIANCE

VOLUME EFFICIENCY VARIANCE

OVERHEAD PRICE VARIANCE

OVERHEAD EFFICIENCY VARIANCE

OVERHEAD UTILISATION VARIANCE

THE VARIANCES ABOVE THE LINE ARE CONSIDERED IN DETAIL

SOURCE "Terminology of Cost Accounting" published by The Institute of Cost and Works Accountants.

The calculation of the variances is as follows:

Materials cost variance—

$$SC - AC$$

Standard cost = Actual production (i.e. 1,100) × Standard cost/unit

$$\left(i.e. \frac{\text{Standard cost per lb.}}{\text{Standard output per lb.}} \frac{\text{£0·5}}{10} = \text{£0·05} \right)$$

= 1,100 × £0·05 = £55

SC − AC

£55 − £45 = £10 favourable

Price variance—

$$AQ\ (SP - AP)$$
$$100\ \text{lb. (£0·5} - \text{£0·45)}$$
$$100 \times \text{£0·05} = \text{£5 favourable}$$

Usage variance—

$$SP\ (SQ - AQ)$$

$$\text{Standard quantity} = \frac{\text{Actual quantity}}{\text{Standard output}} = \frac{1,100}{10} = 110$$

£0·5 (110 − 100) = £5 favourable

Check—

	£
Price variance	5 favourable
Usage variance	5 favourable
Total material variance	£10 favourable

It is possible to illustrate the principles of variance analysis diagrammatically and this is illustrated on page 83. Assume that the standard price of material is £0·6 per pound and that each unit uses 0·5 lb. of material. The actual price of the material was £0·5 per lb. and the actual usage was 0·6 lb. per unit.

The price variance is represented by the quadrant A, i.e.:

$$\text{£0·1} \times 0·5 = \text{£0·05 favourable}$$

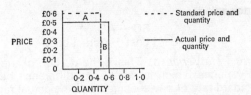

The usage variance is represented by quadrant B, i.e.:

$$£0·5 × 0·1 = £0·05 \text{ unfavourable}$$

The net result is:

	£
Price variance	0·05 favourable
Usage variance	0·05 unfavourable
Total variance	Nil

This result can be checked from the information contained in the example:

	£
Standard cost £0·6 × 0·5	= 0·3 per unit
Actual cost £0·5 × 0·6	= 0·3 per unit
Variance	Nil

This example does illustrate the value of breaking down a total variance, in this case the material variance, into its component parts. The total variance is nil but the breakdown reveals an unfavourable usage variance for which management will require an explanation.

This diagrammatic presentation reveals its limitations when both variances are favourable, and it is better to master the formula approach to variance analysis to avoid these limitations.

Direct Wages Variance

This is the difference between the standard wages specified for the operation and the actual wages paid.

The formula is:

$$SC - AC$$
(Standard cost − Actual cost)

Wages Rate Variance. This is the portion of the direct wages variance which is due to the difference between the standard rate of pay specified and the actual rate paid (this is the equivalent of a price variance).

The formula is:

$$AH (SR - AR)$$
(Actual hours (Standard rate − Actual rate))

Labour Efficiency Variance. This is the portion of the direct wages variance which is due to the difference in the standard labour hours specified for the operation and the actual hours taken.

The formula is:

$$SR (SH - AH)$$
(Standard rate (Standard hours − Actual hours))

Let us consider an example to illustrate these wage variances. The standard time for producing 10 units is 2 hours and the standard rate of pay is £0·75 per hour. During the relevant period 1,100 articles were produced and the wages paid were 200 hours at £0·7 per hour.
Wages Variance:

$$SC - AC$$

Standard cost = actual output at standard rate/units
            = 1,100 × £0·15 = £165
£165 − £140 = £25 favourable variance

Rate Variance:

$$AH (SR - AR)$$
200 (£0·75 − £0·70) = £10 favourable

Efficiency Variance:

$$SR (SH - AH)$$

Standard hour = $\dfrac{\text{Actual output}}{\text{Standard output per hour}} = \dfrac{1,100}{5}$
               = 220
£0·75 (220 − 200) = £15 favourable

Check:

	£
Rate variance	10 favourable
Efficiency variance	15 favourable
Total wage variance	25 favourable

One point which must be considered when calculating wages variances is idle time. Although an allowance will have been made for this when the standard hour was calculated it would not cover such abnormal happenings as prolonged machine breakdowns. If separate account is not taken for these periods employees may be blamed for an adverse efficiency variance which was in fact nothing to do with them. If in the above example the 200 actual hours included 10 hours idle time, then an adverse idle variance would arise calculated as follows:

Idle hours × Standard rate
10 × £0·75 = £7·5 adverse

This would increase the efficiency variance by a similar amount, i.e. from £15 favourable to £22·5 favourable.

Overhead Variances

We have already made a distinction between fixed overheads and variable overheads and variances are calculated for both types of overhead expense. The variable overhead is fairly straighforward as it will vary more or less directly with output.

Variable Overhead Variance. The formula is:

SC − AC
(Standard cost − Actual cost)

Example: The standard variable overhead is £0·4 per unit. During the period the actual variable overhead expenses incurred were £500, and the actual production was 1,100 units.

SC − AC
£440 − £500 = £60 adverse

Fixed Overhead Variances. These variances are probably the most difficult ones to appreciate and they have the largest number of any of the variances. Fixed overheads imply that the expenses do not vary with changes in the level of production unless there is a deliberate change of policy by management. They include such items as depreciation, rent, rates, salaries, etc., and they will not vary whether the output is 70% of capacity or 95%. The amount of overhead recovered will depend on the output, however, and the difference between the amount of overhead charged to output and the actual overhead expenses incurred will result in over- or under-recovery of fixed overhead.

Cost Variance. This is the difference between the overhead recovered at standard rates and the actual overhead incurred.

The formula is:

$$SC - AC$$
(Standard cost − Actual cost)

Volume Variance. This is the portion which is due to the differences between the budgeted and actual output at standard overhead rates.

The formula is:

$$SR (AQ - BQ)$$
(Standard rate (Actual quantity − Budgeted quantity))

Expenditure Variance. This is the portion of the cost variance which is due to differences between the budgeted overhead for the period and the actual overhead incurred.

The formula is:

$$BC - AC$$
(Budgeted cost − Actual cost)

Efficiency Variance. This is the difference between the actual quantity of units produced and the standard quantity which should have been produced multiplied by the standard overhead rate.

The formula is:

$$SR (AQ - SQ)$$
(Standard rate (Actual quantity − Standard quantity))

Capacity Variance. This is the difference between the budgeted quantity and the standard quantity multiplied by the standard rate. (Such a difference will usually be due to fewer hours being worked than expected, e.g. if the budgeted output for a 40-hour week is 1,000 units and the standard output per hour is 25 units, then, if through idle time only 38 hours are worked in a particular week, the number of units which should be produced in the time available is 38 × 25, i.e. 950 units.)

The formula is:

$$SR (SQ - BQ)$$
(Standard rate (Standard quantity − Budgeted quantity))

Both the efficiency and the capacity variance are sub-variances of the volume variance. The relationships are illustrated in the diagram below which forms part of the total cost variance diagram appearing on page 81.

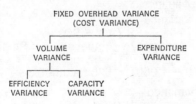

Let us now see how these variances work out in a practical problem.

Example: During a period the budgeted output was 1,000 units, 20,000 units being the budgeted output for the year at a budgeted fixed overhead of £5,000. Standard performance is 5 units per hour and the actual fixed overheads were £330. The actual hours worked were 200 and the actual output was 1,100 units.

Fixed overhead variance (cost variance):

$$SC - AC$$

Standard cost = Actual output × Standard rate
$$= 1,100 \times £0 \cdot 25$$
$$= £275$$

£275 − £330 = £55 adverse

$$\left(\text{Standard rate is found by } \frac{\text{Budgeted fixed overhead}}{\text{Budgeted output}} \right)$$

Volume variance:

$$SR (AQ - BQ)$$
$$£0 \cdot 25 (1,100 - 1,000) = £25 \text{ favourable}$$

Expenditure variance:

$$BC - AC$$
$$£250 - £330 = £80 \text{ adverse}$$

Check:

	£
Volume variance	25 favourable
Expenditure variance	80 adverse
Fixed overhead variance	55 adverse

Sub-volume variances:

  Efficiency variance—

$$SR (AQ - SQ)$$

Standard quantity = Actual hours × Standard quantity per hour
$$£0 \cdot 25 (1,100 - 1,000) = £25 \text{ favourable}$$

  Capacity variance—

$$SR (SQ - BQ)$$
$$£0 \cdot 25 (1,000 - 1,000) = 0$$

Check:

	£
Efficiency variance	25 favourable
Capacity variance	0
Volume variance	25 favourable

You will have, no doubt, noticed that the examples used to illustrate each of the main variances, i.e. materials, labour and overhead, are related and we can now consider the complete problem.

Summarised problem:

During a particular period the following standards and estimates were in operation—

    1 lb. of material will produce 10 articles
    Standard price of material is £0·50
    Standard time for producing 10 articles is 2 hours
    Standard rate of pay is £0·75 per hour
    Budgeted output is 1,000 units
    Budgeted variable overhead is £0·4 per unit
    Budgeted fixed overhead £250

The following actual costs, etc., were incurred during this period—

    100 lb. of material was issued at a cost of £0·45 per lb.
    Actual production was 1,100 articles
    200 hours were worked at a cost of £0·7 per hour
    Variable overhead expenses were £500
    Fixed overhead expenses were £330

The basic variances may be summarised by the following tables. These are the figures which have been calculated earlier in this chapter using the relevant formulae.

Variance	Adverse	Fav.	Net ±
	£	£	£
Direct materials			
Price		5	
Usage		5	10+
Direct wages			
Rate		10	
Efficiency		15	25+
Variable overhead	60		60−
Fixed overhead			
Volume		25	
Expenditure	80		55−
Total cost variance			£80 adverse

This total cost variance can also be checked by comparing the actual costs with the standards for the actual output.

Cost Element	Standard		Actual	Variance	
	Per article	Per output 1,100 articles		Fav.	Adv.
	£	£	£	£	£
Materials	0·05	55	45	10	
Labour	0·15	165	140	25	
Variable overhead	0·4	440	500		60
Fixed overhead	0·25	275	330		55
	0·85	£935	£1,015	£35	£115
Net					£80

Management must be presented with the results produced by the standard costing system as quickly as possible if the full benefits of utilising such a system are to be obtained and the necessary action to correct variances must be taken immediately.

The statement presented to management would be as follows for our example, assuming that sales are £1,235.

Profit and Loss Statement for the Period Ending 31/x/xx

	£	£
Sales (actual)		1,235
Less Standard cost of sales		
Materials	55	
Labour	165	
Overhead	715	935
Standard net profit		£300

Variances:
(The table on the previous page would be produced here)—

Total cost variance	£80 adverse
Actual net profit	£220

From this statement management is able to see that profit for the period was £80 less than anticipated mainly owing to the actual variable and fixed overhead expenses being more than the estimated amounts.

Explanations for these variances should be obtained from the buyer etc. and appropriate action taken to remedy the situation. It may be that the standards for these variances require amending.

Sales Variances

Many companies which have installed a standard cost system restrict it to showing the effects on profits of adverse or favourable variances of labour, materials and overhead costs. However, a complete system should also produce sales variances.

There are two methods for calculating sales variances and their results are not compatible. One method shows the effect of a change in sales on turnover and the basic variance is found by taking the actual sales from the budgeted sales, i.e. BS − AS. This basic variance is composed of two sub-variances, i.e. volume variance represented by (*a*) Budgeted sales − Standard sales and (*b*) a price variance represented by Standard selling price − Actual selling price.

The other method shows the effect of a change in sales on profits rather than turnover. The basic variance is calculated by the formula, Budgeted profit − Actual profit, and again the two components of this basic variance are volume, represented by Budgeted profit − Standard profit, and price, represented by Standard profit − Actual profit.

It is not proposed to show a detailed example, as the calculations using the above formula are quite straightforward. The only items which perhaps require an explanation are standard sales and standard profit. Standard sales are calculated by multiplying the actual sales in units by the standard or budgeted price per unit and standard profit is found by multiplying the actual quantity by the standard or budgeted profit per unit.

The variances not considered in detail in this chapter, e.g. material mix and yield, overhead calendar, etc., are rather complicated and beyond the scope of this book. If further information on these variances is required, suitable texts will be found in the bibliography at the end of this book.

Questions

1. Outline the main advantages of standard costing.

2. Consider the three broad categories of the word "standard" as applied to standard costing.

3. What are the two main types of variance?

4. Draw up a cost variance analysis chart.

5. The material variance is made up of the . . . . . . variance and the . . . . . . variance.

6. How will idle time affect the direct labour variance?

7. What are the components of the fixed overhead variance?

8. Design a suitable statement for presenting variances to management.

9. Briefly outline the two main methods of calculating sales variances.

10. What system might be used to amend basic standards to keep them up to date?

Chapter 8

MARGINAL COSTING AND COST–PROFIT–VOLUME RELATIONSHIPS

Definition

The Institute of Cost and Works Accountants defines marginal cost as "the amount at any given volume of output by which aggregate costs are changed if the volume of output is increased or decreased by one unit" and marginal costing as "the ascertainment, by differentiating between fixed costs and variable costs, of marginal costs and of the effect on profit of changes in volume or type of output".

The whole subject of marginal costing has created a great deal of contention among accountants and economists. One tends to be either wholly for the system or wholly against it and a great deal has been written on both sides of the question.

Marginal costing is a technique which enables management to consider costs in a different and, it is claimed, a more meaningful light, particularly from the point of view of the profitability of different products. A conventional costing system would allocate all costs (i.e. direct and overhead) to the units produced and would ascertain whether the sales exceeded these total costs. Marginal costing differentiates between variable and fixed costs. Fixed costs are charged in total to the profit and loss account as they are the type of costs, e.g. rent, insurance, rates, clerical costs, subscriptions, which normally relate to a specific period of time, and it is felt that they should be recovered during the current period and not depend upon recovery according to the volume of units produced during the period, as this is likely to result in under- or over-recovery.

One reason why fixed costs are eliminated is the effect

which they can have on pricing policies if they are tied to recovery on a volume basis. Consider a factory incurring £2,000 of fixed costs per week and producing 2,000 articles. If fixed costs are recovered on a volume basis, this will result in an overhead charge of £1 per unit. Next week the fixed cost will still be £2,000, but if the production is now 3,000 units the fixed costs will now be recovered at a rate of £0·67; and if the following week a breakdown results in only 500 units being produced the £2,000 fixed costs will be recovered at £4 per unit. Although these are wide variations, even with minor fluctuations in output, price fixing can be a difficult problem.

Fixed/Variable Costs Classification

If fixed costs are eliminated from the cost computations, then we are left with variable costs, which are those costs which tend to vary in direct proportion to the number of units produced. It would, therefore, seem relatively easy to use a marginal costing system, and the advantages appear to be considerable. The main drawback is, however, in deciding which costs are fixed and which are variable. Certain costs are easily classified; e.g. all direct costs (i.e. direct materials, direct wages and direct expenses) are obviously variable costs, and similarly the fixed costs outlined above are easily classifiable. But there are a number of overhead costs which might be called semi-variable or semi-fixed, and unless some fairly accurate method is used to put these into their correct category the whole procedure is likely to go wrong. Examples of these semi-fixed variable costs are power and light, inspection and repairs and maintenance.

Methods of Dividing Semi-variable Overheads into Fixed and Variable Elements

There are three basic methods of producing such a division; but as we are concerned with the accuracy of the split, only the most reliable will be explained in detail.

The three methods are;

  (a) the range method;
  (b) the scatter diagram;
  (c) the method of least squares.

Method (a) relies on listing high and low levels of observed overhead costs and then using the figures to calculate a rather unscientific division between fixed and variable costs. Method (b) is more accurate but relies on a "best-fit" line, i.e. a line which is drawn through a number of points plotted on a graph so as to pass through as many as possible. It is therefore open to subjective manipulation by the compiler. Method (c) is likely to give the most accurate separation into fixed and variable elements but it is naturally the most complicated of the three, involving the use of a formula. However, it is not necessary to know the derivation of a formula before one can use it and we shall take the formula as read and just consider how it can be applied to a specific problem.

Problem. The following figures for the six-month period July to December show the cost of heating and the number of units produced, heat being an integral part of the production process as well as being a general amenity:

	1	2
Month	*Heating costs*	*Units produced*
	£	£
July	500	1,300
August	700	1,600
September	600	1,100
October	700	1,500
November	800	1,600
December	900	1,300
	£4,200	£8,400

Average monthly cost of heating $\dfrac{£4,200}{6}$ = £700 (A)

Average monthly production $\dfrac{8,400}{6}$ = 1,400 (B)

Average cost of heating per unit = £0·5

Month	3	4	5	6
	(1 − A)	(2 − B)	(4²)	(3 × 4)
July	−200	−100	10,000	+20,000
August	—	+200	40,000	—
September	−100	−300	90,000	+30,000
October	—	+100	10,000	—
November	+100	+200	40,000	+20,000
December	+200	−100	10,000	−20,000
	—	—	200,000	+50,000

The variable element of the heating cost is found by:

$$\frac{\text{Column 6}}{\text{Column 5}} = \frac{50,000}{200,000} = £0.25$$

The fixed cost will therefore also be £0·25.

Value of Marginal Costing

Having established the basic idea of marginal costing as the allocation of costs into fixed and variable, let us now see how this system can be of value to management.

If the marginal costs are deducted from the sales the difference is known as the contribution. This contribution is available to meet the pool of fixed costs, and the surplus after these have been met is net profit.

This situation can be illustrated by a simple formula.

    1. Sales − Variable costs = Contribution.
    2. Contribution − Fixed costs = Profit.
    3. ∴ Sales − Variable costs = Fixed costs + Profit.

If the result of (1) is positive, i.e. there is something available to meet fixed costs, it may be worth continuing production even though under an absorption costing system the product appears to be making a loss.

Consider the example on page 97.

From this statement if would appear that if sales of Product C cannot be increased the only alternative would be to cease production of this product and thereby make an apparent saving of £1,000. However, the £1,000 loss might well be due to the manner in which fixed overhead costs have been apportioned between the products. As

*Budgeted Trading Statement for the Six Months Ending
31st December 19xx*

	Total	A	B	C
			Product	
	£	£	£	£
Prime costs and variable overheads	15,000	6,000	5,000	4,000
Fixed costs	7,000	3,000	2,000	2,000
Total cost	22,000	9,000	7,000	6,000
Sales	29,000	14,000	10,000	5,000
Profit	7,000	5,000	3,000	
Loss				£1,000

this is usually a very arbitrary decision a much more revealing picture is shown if the statement is produced on a
marginal costing basis. This is shown below.

*Marginal Trading Statement for the Six Months Ending
31st December 19xx*

	Total	A	B	C
			Product	
	£	£	£	£
Sales	29,000	14,000	10,000	5,000
Less Variable costs	15,000	6,000	5,000	4,000
Contribution	14,000	8,000	5,000	1,000
Less Fixed costs	7,000			
Profit	£7,000			

It will be seen that Product C makes a contribution to
the fixed costs of £1,000.

If Product C is eliminated this is likely to have little
effect on the fixed costs. These will, therefore, now have
to be borne by the other two products and the profit is
reduced by £1,000 from £7,000 to £6,000. This is
illustrated on page 98.

	Total	Product A	Product B
	£	£	£
Sales	24,000	14,000	10,000
Less Variable costs	11,000	6,000	5,000
Contribution	13,000	8,000	5,000
Less Fixed costs	7,000		
Profit	£6,000		

Advantages and Disadvantages of Marginal Costing
Advantages

1. It is not necessary to allocate fixed overhead expenses to cost centres and problems of over- and under-recovery of overheads are eliminated.

2. Management, when concerned with price fixing, finds the marginal cost statement much easier to understand.

3. Marginal costs per unit are not generally affected by changes in volume of output.

4. The contribution which each product makes towards fixed overheads and profits is easily ascertained. This is useful in times of a trade recession, when maximisation of profit is not always possible and any orders which cover marginal costs are worth having.

5. The exclusion of fixed overhead costs from stock and work in progress valuations gives more uniform and realistic figures.

Disadvantages

1. The allocation of semi-variable costs into their variable and fixed element is a complicated procedure if accuracy is required.

2. Short-term pricing may take account of the contribution of individual products and production of some products may continue when the contribution is insufficient to meet the fixed overheads. This can, however, only be a temporary measure as in the long run all fixed overheads

must be covered and a reasonable margin obtained over and above total costs.

3. Although it is not necessary to allocate fixed overheads, it is still necessary to allocate variable overheads to cost centres.

4. Difficulties arise in the contracting industries such as shipbuilding. It is often necessary to value work in progress at total cost and calculate a profit element to appear in the annual accounts in order to avoid large fluctuations in profits which would occur if profit was only recorded when the revenue was received (i.e. on completion of the contract). Under a marginal costing system this valuation would be very difficult.

Cost–Profit–Volume Relationships

It is vitally necessary that management should be aware of the effect of volume of output upon profits. This is particularly so when a new product is being introduced or there is a slump in the industry resulting in reduced sales. Once costs have been grouped into fixed and variable, then it is possible to show the relationship between sales and output, and more specifically at what output total costs equal sales. At this point there will be neither profits nor losses, and this is known as the break-even point.

We can use the simple relationship already established, i.e.:

Sales − Variable costs = Fixed costs + Profit

to produce a formula which will calculate this break-even point.

Units required to break-even =
$$\frac{\text{Fixed costs}}{\text{Selling price} - \text{Variable costs per unit}}$$

If the sales revenue needed to break-even is required, then it can be found by the formula:

$$\frac{\text{Fixed costs} \times \text{Sales}}{\text{Sales} - \text{Variable costs}}$$

Let us see how these formulae work on a practical question. During a particular year the following estimates were made:

Fixed costs, £15,000
Prime costs, £3 per unit
Variable overheads, £2 per unit
Number of units to be produced, 10,000
Selling price per unit, £8.

How many units must be produced to break-even?
Formula:

$$\frac{FC}{SP - VCU}$$

$$= \frac{£15,000}{£8 - £3} = \frac{£15,000}{£3} = 5,000 \text{ units}$$

The equivalent sales revenue needed to break-even may be found by multiplying the units figure above by the selling price, i.e. 5,000 × £8 = £40,000. It may also be found by the formula:

$$\frac{FC \times S}{S - VC} = \frac{£15,000 \times £80,000}{£80,000 - £50,000} = \frac{£120,000}{£3} = £40,000$$

The significance of these figures, i.e. 5,000 units and £40,000 sales revenue is that the company must achieve this sales level before it starts to make a profit. If these figures are not achieved a loss will occur.

It is generally easier for management to appreciate the significance of cost–profit–volume relationships if they are presented in graphical form. This is known as a break-even chart and preparation of such a chart is fairly straight-forward. The left-hand vertical side of the chart is known as the Y axis and the horizontal side at the bottom is the X axis.

It is usual to show costs and revenues on the Y axis and volume either in units or £s on the X axis. Capacity in percentage terms may be an alternative X axis notation.

The figures already given will now be plotted on such a chart on the following page.

BREAK EVEN CHART I

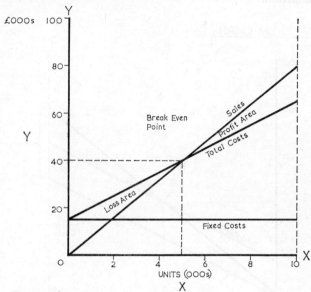

Preparation

1. The fixed cost line is firstly drawn in at £15,000. This will be horizontal as fixed costs do not vary with volume of output.

2. The total cost line can now be plotted. This represents an increase in costs of £5 for each unit produced (note the line starts at the fixed cost point on the Y axis).

3. The sales revenue at £8 per unit is then plotted.

4. The break-even point lies on the intersection of the total sales and total cost line. Losses are measured to the left of the break-even point, the amount of loss in £s at any point being equal to the difference between the total cost line and the total sales line. Profits are measured to the right of the point, the amount being calculated in a similar manner.

Another method of presenting this information is by using the contribution concept already considered. This is illustrated in Chart II below, using the same figures as in the last chart.

BREAK EVEN CHART II

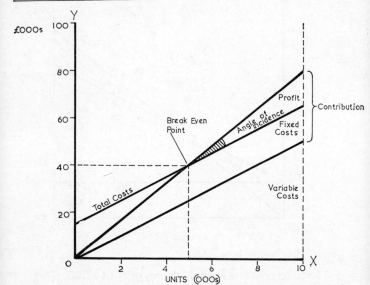

It is claimed that this type of chart reveals more clearly the effects of fixed overheads on the volume of sales.

It will be appreciated that the information which can be shown on such a chart is extremely varied. Consider the very composite chart (Chart III) on page 103.

The desired profit could be further split into the amount needed to finance the capital of the concern, i.e. debenture interest, preference share dividend, ordinary dividend and retained earnings.

Two important points revealed by the conventional break-even chart are the margin of safety and the angle of incidence.

Margin of Safety. This is the difference between the total sales figure and the amount of sales at break-even

BREAK EVEN CHART III

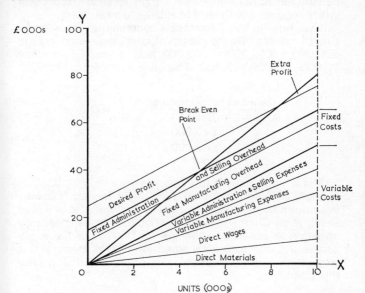

UNITS (000s)

point. It may be expressed as a percentage based either on units or £ value. It is important that there should be a reasonable margin of safety, because otherwise a reduced level of output might mean that the firm was unable to break-even and losses were incurred. Consider the following situation:

	Firm A	Firm B
	£	£
Total sales	50,000	80,000
Break-even point	30,000	64,000
Margin of safety	£20,000	£16,000
Margin of safety as a percentage of sales	40%	20%

If the rate of profit earned on sales above break-even point is the same, Company A is in a much stronger position than Company B to withstand a fall in sales. A low percentage usually indicates a high level of fixed costs which requires a high level of activity to cover them.

If we refer to the information contained in Break-even Chart I we see that the margin of safety expressed in £s is £80,000 − £40,000 = £40,000 and expressed in units 10,000 − 5,000 = 5,000. This gives a percentage of 50%, i.e.:

$$\frac{\text{Sales at break-even point}}{\text{Sales}} \times 100$$
$$= \frac{£40,000}{£80,000} \times 100$$
$$= 50\%$$

This is a highly satisfactory margin.

Angle of Incidence. This is the angle formed at break-even point by the sales line cutting the total cost line (see Break-even Chart II). The aim should be to have as large an angle as possible at this point. The size of the angle shows the rate of profit earned after break-even, and a large angle will mean a high rate of profit accruing after this point.

Profit–Volume Chart

This type of chart is sometimes used in place of or in addition to a break-even chart. Profits and losses are shown on the vertical scale and units or percentage of capacity are shown on the horizontal scale. The profits and losses at various sales levels are then plotted on the chart and where this line crosses the horizontal zero line this is the break-even point.

Let us see how our original example would be presented on such a chart which can be found on page 105.

The advantage of such a chart is that it is possible to read off the profit or loss at any given level of production, but it does not show how costs vary with any given activity.

Management are able to use break-even analysis for short-term planning on the assumption that market prices are established and that moderate changes in output will

CHART IV

PROFIT/ VOLUME CHART

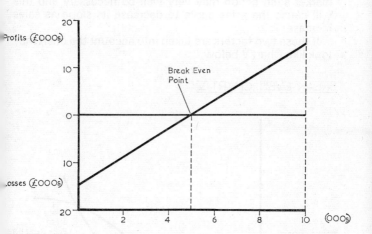

not affect the price. In the long run other factors may be taken into account; e.g. it may be decided to sacrifice immediate profits by producing beyond the point of maximum profit, in order to secure a market that will yield greater profits when additional capacity is available.

Limitations of Break-even Analysis

One of the basic faults of the simple break-even chart is that it is assumed that the total sales line and the total cost line are straight, i.e. linear. It is unlikely to be the case in practice as there will come a point when the addition of variable factors of production to a given fixed factor will result in reduced efficiency. This follows from the economists' Law of Diminishing Returns. The total cost line is likely, therefore, to have an increasing slope as more is produced. It may also follow that at low levels of production, efficiency may be increasing, thus causing the slope of the total cost curve to be decreasing at that particular level of production.

When the sales line is plotted as a straight line it is assumed that it will not be necessary to decrease the unit price in order to achieve more sales; but in a competitive market such action may very well be necessary and this will cause the sales curve to decrease its slope as sales increase.

If these two factors are taken into account the chart may look like Chart V below.

BREAK EVEN CHART V

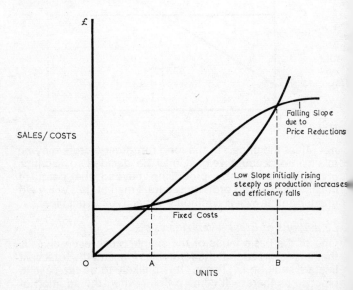

It will be observed that there are two break-even points at *OA* and *OB*. This is due to having curved lines instead of the usual straight ones. Optimum output, i.e. that at which maximum profitability will be achieved, is where the sales curve and total cost curve are farthest apart, i.e. where the difference between total expenses and total sales is greatest.

Although fixed costs have so far always been shown as a straight line even these will vary as production increases. Such costs will normally remain unchanged until a certain limit of capacity is reached and when they do change it will be in definite jumps, or steps rather than gradually. For example, if capacity is increased by the purchase of a new factory, then there will be an immediate rise in fixed costs to take account of the increased rates, heating, depreciation, etc. However, as the main use of break-even analysis is for short-term planning it is permissible to show fixed costs as being unchanged throughout the short term.

Despite these limitations, the simple break-even chart does enable cost–volume–profit relationships to be clearly shown. And as the normal business will be working within a limited range of production the straight lines, although only approximating to the actual position, will be sufficiently accurate to provide adequate information for management's decision-making.

Summary

Historical, marginal and standard costing systems are not mutually exclusive, i.e. you may have, and in a large organisation you should have, all three systems in operation.

Marginal costing will aid the initial decision, e.g. whether to increase production or make or buy a component.

Standard costing will allow targets to be established and historical costing will enable the actual results to be compared with the pre-determined standards.

Questions

1. Define marginal costing.
2. Consider the three main methods of dividing semi-variable overheads into fixed and variable elements.
3. What do you understand by the term "contribution"?
4. Complete the following equation:

$$\text{Sales} - \text{Variable costs} = \ldots\ldots\ldots + \text{Profit}$$

5. In what circumstances might a firm be willing to sell at a price below its total costs?

6. Give the formula for calculating sales at break-even point and number of units at break-even point.

7. Prepare a break-even chart from the following information for a period:

> Selling price, £5 per unit
> Number of units produced, 5,000
> Fixed overheads, £5,000
> Variable costs, £3 per unit

8. What is the margin of safety? Calculate the margin in units from the figures in the last question.

9. From the information contained in question 7 prepare a profit–volume chart and explain its significance.

10. What are the limitations of break-even analysis?

Chapter 9

ACCOUNTING RATIOS

Ratios Used in Financial Analysis and Interpretation of Accounts

The published accounts of a concern may be used by different people for different purposes. They are, of course, primarily an account of the stewardship function of management which they are obliged to prepare for the owners of the company, i.e. the shareholders. However, the accounts will also prove invaluable to the financial analyst who is acting as an investment adviser, or to the bank manager who has been requested to give a loan or overdraft facilities to the company, or even to the prospective creditor of the company in order that he might assess the creditworthiness of the company before selling goods to them. Management will also be able to ascertain meaningful ratios from the published accounts. (However, they also have access to unpublished information which may, from their point of view, be even more valuable.) Management ratios will be considered in the next chapter.

Limitations

Over-emphasis of a single ratio should be avoided and it is essential to look at the following points when considering individual ratios. First, how does the particular ratio fit in with the trend over the past few years; secondly, how does the ratio compare with other ratios obtained from the same set of information; finally, what influence does the type of business activity have on the ratio. For example, we might expect a low current assets to fixed assets ratio if we were considering the accounts of a market stallholder where the only fixed asset might be a motor vehicle for transporting his stock; but such a ratio would not be acceptable for a motor-car manufacturer.

Ratios Obtained from the Balance Sheet

We will use the following balance sheet to illustrate the various ratios.

Balance Sheet as at 31st December 19xx

	£		£	£
80,000 ordinary shares (£1)	80,000	*Fixed Assets*		
5% preference shares (£1)	60,000	Buildings	100,000	
General reserve	10,000	Plant and machinery	50,000	
Profit and loss a/c balance	10,000	Fixtures and fittings	30,000	
				180,000
	160,000			
7% Debentures	60,000			
Current Liabilities		*Current Assets*		
	£			
Creditors	12,000	Stock	35,000	
Taxation	17,000	Debtors	19,000	
Dividend	11,000	Bank	26,000	
	40,000			80,000
	£260,000			£260,000

Share Valuation

Although there are a number of methods which may be adopted to value shares we shall use the asset valuation method. This involves calculating the total equity of the company, i.e. that part of the capital which has been subscribed for by the ordinary shareholders plus retained earnings.

In our example we have:

	£
Ordinary shares of £1 each	80,000
General reserve	10,000
Profit and loss A/c. balance	10,000
Equity	£100,000

Asset value of 1 ordinary share— $\dfrac{£100,000}{80,000} = £1\cdot25$

The same result will occur if the current liabilities, debentures and preference shares are deducted from the total assets. The benefit of doing the calculation in this way is that the assets can be valued on a realistic basis rather than as shown in the balance sheet. Thus some of the fixed assets, e.g. buildings, may be worth more than the balance sheet figure ; and account can also be taken of the fact that current assets must be used effectively if their full value is to be taken in the calculation. For example, a large cash balance accumulated for no particular purpose cannot be said to be effectively employed in the business, and this fact would be taken into account when arriving at the total asset figure for the computation.

The computed figure may be compared with the actual Stock Exchange quotation, if the company is quoted ; but this can only be a very general guide, as stock market prices are influenced by many external factors not directly related to the performance of companies.

Liquidity Ratios

It is possible for a concern to be earning a high rate of profit yet still encounter difficulties in meeting its day-to-day commitments. This is known as "overtrading".

The two ratios to ascertain the availability of funds are :

(*a*) current ratio ;
(*b*) quick assets or liquid ratio.

The current ratio assesses the overall working capital position and is found by :

$$\frac{\text{Current assets}}{\text{Current liabilities}}$$

In our example this would be :

$$\frac{£80,000}{£40,000} = 2:1$$

This result might be said to be the perfect ratio as this ratio has been called "the 2:1 ratio". However, high ratios may be the result of poor investment policies or too large a holding of stock ; and it is necessary to consider carefully the type of business under analysis and also the result of the other ratio concerned with liquidity, i.e. the quick ratio.

The quick ratio demonstrates the ability of the concern to meet its immediate commitments. It is frequently called the acid test ratio. Stock may take a large share of the total current assets, yet in an emergency it will probably be difficult to transform it quickly into cash and if it has to be sold under such circumstances it is likely to yield far less than its book value. To calculate the quick ratio, stock is taken away from the total current assets to give liquid assets.

In our example this will result in

$$\frac{£45,000}{£40,000} = 1 \cdot 125 : 1$$

This ratio should generally be at least 1 : 1 and if it is below this figure immediate steps should be taken to obtain cash.

It can be very damaging to the future activities of the business if it cannot pay its immediate liabilities. Creditors will be less willing in the future to sell goods to the company on credit and in extreme cases of insolvency the company may be forced into liquidation.

Net Current Assets to Fixed Assets

As already mentioned this ratio will depend upon the type of business being analysed. It is most useful if it is compared with the same ratio ascertained for other businesses involved in the same type of activity. However, comparisons may be misleading due to different policies adopted by different managements; e.g. frequent revaluation of fixed assets by one company, or different depreciation rates being used by different companies.

Our example would yield:

$$\frac{£40,000}{£180,000} = 1 : 4 \cdot 5$$

Proprietors Ratio

The proprietor should provide sufficient capital to cover the fixed assets and some part of the working capital. If this is not done, then reliance will have to be placed on outside financing and this may involve undesirable conditions being imposed by the lenders.

The proprietors ratio is:

$$\frac{\text{Capital employed}}{\text{Liabilities (short- and long-term)}}$$

The capital employed for the purpose of this ratio comprises the original capital, all types of share being included, plus the amounts which have been retained in the business for future expansion.

Our example gives us:

$$\frac{£160,000}{£100,000 \text{ (i.e. Current liabilities + Debentures)}} = 1·6:1$$

Subsequent calculation of this ratio will reveal whether there has been an increase or decrease in the funds being supplied by outsiders or whether finance is being provided from internal sources.

Capital Employed to Fixed Assets

Ideally the owners of the business should "cover" all the fixed assets and part of the current assets. This was outlined for the last ratio. The capital employed to fixed assets ratio reveals whether any part of the fixed assets are owned by debenture holders or other creditors.

In our example the ratio is:

$$\frac{£160,000}{£180,000} = 1:1·125$$

which does in fact mean that some of the fixed assets have been financed by outside lenders.

Gearing Ratio

Gearing has already been considered in some detail in Chapter 3 and therefore we shall just calculate the ratio for our particular company.

$$\text{Capital gearing ratio} = \frac{\text{Ordinary share capital}}{\text{Fixed interest capital}}$$

$$= \frac{£80,000}{£120,000} = 0·66:1$$

This low ratio shows our company to be highly geared, i.e. one which has a high proportion of fixed interest capital. This will mean that equity earnings will rise and fall faster than, and hence disproportionately to, variations in total profits.

Ratios Utilising the Trading Account and Profit and Loss Account

These ratios are often termed operating ratios and we shall use the following Trading Account and Profit and Loss Account in conjunction with the Balance Sheet already given.

Trading Account for the Year Ending 31st December 19xx

	£	£		£
Opening stock	15,000		Sales	365,000
Purchases	315,000			
	———	330,000		
Less Closing stock		35,000		
		———		
		295,000		
Gross profit c/d		70,000		
		———		———
		£365,000		£365,000

Profit and Loss Account for the Year Ending 31st December 19xx

	£		£
Administration expenses	12,000	Gross profit b/d	70,000
Selling expenses	8,000		
Distribution expenses	5,000		
Financial expenses	10,000		
Net profit c/f	35,000		
	———		———
	£70,000		£70,000

Profit and Loss Appropriation Account for the Year Ending 31st December 19xx

	£		£
Dividend	11,000	Net profit b/d	35,000
Transfer to reserve	2,000	Balance brought	
Taxation	17,000	forward	5,000
Balance carried to balance			
sheet	10,000		
	———		———
	£40,000		£40,000

Credit Sales to Debtors Ratio

This ratio reveals how quickly the cash is being received from credit sales. The ratio should have a definite relationship to the period of credit allowed to customers, thus if customers are allowed 30 days to pay, then this would mean a ratio of 12:1, i.e. 365 days divided by 30.

In our example sales are £365,000 and debtors £19,000. The ratio is:

$$\frac{£365,000}{£19,000} = 19:1,$$

which is a high ratio indicating that debtors pay their accounts very quickly.

To establish the average collection period the sales are divided by 365 to obtain the average daily sales and this is then divided into the debtors to give the average collection period i.e.

$$\frac{Debtors}{Sales \div 365} = \frac{£19,000}{£365,000 \div 365}$$
$$= 19 \text{ days}$$

It is obviously of great benefit to the business if money can be collected as quickly as this, i.e. just under three weeks on average.

Purchases to Creditors Ratio

A similar ratio can be calculated for creditors. This will show on average how quickly the business is settling its own debts.

The ratio is:

$$\frac{Purchases}{Creditors} = \frac{£315,000}{£12,000} = 26:1$$

The average payment period is found by:

$$\frac{Creditors}{Purchases \div 365} = \frac{£12,000}{£315,000 \div 365} = 14 \text{ days}$$

Both of the last two ratios reveal very short intervals for payment of creditors and receiving money from debtors. A more usual figure of one month might be expected, but this will be influenced by discounts given for prompt payment both by the business and by its creditors.

Sales to Fixed Assets

This ratio shows the efficiency achieved in the use of fixed assets. It is particularly useful for comparison purposes to ascertain whether the sales per £1 of fixed assets is increasing or decreasing over a period.

In our example:

$$\frac{\text{Sales}}{\text{Fixed assets}} = \frac{£365,000}{£180,000} = 2:1$$

Each £1 of fixed assets is producing over £2 of sales. This is a satisfactory position and comparison with previous periods will show whether the trend is favourable or otherwise.

Gross Profit Ratio

This reveals the average mark-up on the cost of goods available for sale. It is essential that this percentage should be sufficiently high to bear the overhead charges and still make a net profit, but it may be influenced by market factors, particularly competition, which will tend to make the rate of mark-up an important management decision.

Our example gives us:

$$\frac{\text{Gross profit}}{\text{Sales}} = \frac{£70,000}{£365,000} \times \frac{100}{1} = 19\% \text{ approximately}$$

If, however, a number of different products are made such an average can be misleading. This was shown in the example in Chapter 1 when only one of the three products manufactured had the same net profit as the average net profit, and the average was in fact masking a product making a substantial loss.

Net Profit Ratio

In this ratio the Net Profit is substituted for Gross Profit i.e.

$$\frac{\text{Net profit}}{\text{Sales}} = \frac{£35,000}{£365,000} \times \frac{100}{1} = 9 \cdot 6\%$$

Stock Turnover Ratio

Here we are concerned with the number of times the average stock is turned over during the year. This indicates how the stock is flowing through the business and is valuable as a guide to present activities compared with past events. If the ratio is increasing this usually means that business is expanding and if it is decreasing, then vice versa. Care must be taken when using the ratio because of the effect which opening and closing stocks have upon it.

The method of calculation is:

$$\frac{\text{Cost of sales}}{\text{Average stock}}$$

Cost of sales in our example consists of:

Opening stock	£15,000	
Purchases	£315,000	
		£330,000
Less Closing stock		£35,000
Cost of sales		£295,000

Average stock is found as follows:

$$\frac{\text{Opening stock} + \text{Closing stock}}{2}$$

i.e. $\dfrac{£15,000 + £35,000}{2} = £25,000$

Turnover ratio is therefore:

$$\frac{£295,000}{£25,000} = \text{Approximately 12 times}$$

This means roughly that the stock is completely turned over on average once a month, and also that the stock-holding period is 4 weeks or more. The influence of opening and closing stocks can be illustrated by the following example.

If the cost of sales remained the same in the next period, but it was decided to hold a stock of £35,000 throughout the year, then the ratio falls to:

$$\frac{£295,000}{£35,000} = \text{Approximately 8 times}$$

The *cost* of holding such stock is an important point which should always be borne in mind when considering how much stock is to be held. This cost is made up of the interest being lost on thecapital tied up in the stock, together with warehouse and storage expenses incurred.

Careful control should be maintained over stock levels, and only sufficient stocks should be held to ensure that production requirements will be met without undue delays.

Expense Ratios

Here we are concerned with the ratio of various overhead expenses to sales, i.e. administration expenses to sales, selling expenses to sales, distribution expenses to sales and financial expenses to sales. By observing the trends in these ratios and the relationships between them it is possible to spot significant changes and assess what action management has taken and should take.

In our example, the ratios are:

			%
Administration expenses to sales	$\frac{£12,000}{£365,000}$	= 1 : 30	3·3
Selling expenses to sales	$\frac{£8,000}{£365,000}$	= 1 : 45	2·2
Distribution expenses to sales	$\frac{£5,000}{£365,000}$	= 1 : 73	1·4
Financial expenses to sales	$\frac{£10,000}{£365,000}$	= 1 : 36	3·7

Financial Ratios for the Investor

It will now be necessary for us to assume a market price for the shares of our company. Let us say the current stock market price is £1·5 per £1 share. We can now calculate a number of important ratios from the investor's point of view.

Dividend Yield. The rate of dividend on ordinary shares is found by deducting the preference share dividend, i.e. £60,000 × 5% = £3,000 from the total dividend paid, i.e. £11,000. This leaves £8,000 for the ordinary shares which is a rate of 10% on the £80,000 ordinary share capital.

By dividing the dividend rate by the market price a more realistic yield is achieved.

This is found by:

$$\frac{\text{Par value of share} \times \text{Dividend \%}}{\text{Market value}}$$

In our example:

$$\frac{£1 \times 10\%}{£1 \cdot 5} = 6 \cdot 7\%$$

It should be noted that the company is required to deduct income tax at the standard rate from all its dividend payments. Such deductions must be paid over to the Inland Revenue within one month.

Dividend Cover. Here we are concerned with how many times the dividend is covered by earnings. This is important to the investor as he can ensure that management are not paying out all earnings or reducing capital (i.e. previous earnings retained) but are pursuing a prudent policy of ploughing back some part of the year's profits.

The formula is:

$$\frac{\text{Profits (after tax)} - \text{Preference dividend}}{\text{Dividend on ordinary shares}}$$

$$= \frac{£35,000 - £17,000 - £3,000}{£8,000}$$

$$= \frac{£15,000}{£8,000} = 1 \cdot 875 \text{ times covered}$$

Price Earnings Ratio. This ratio has come to the fore in recent years as a measure of the relationship between the current market price of the share and earnings.

The earnings per share will be the amount available for the ordinary shareholder to be either paid out as a dividend or retained in the business to promote future growth.

The formula is:

$$\frac{\text{Profit (after tax)} - \text{Preference dividend}}{\text{Number of ordinary shares}}$$

In our example this gives us:

$$\frac{£18,000 - £3,000}{80,000} = \frac{£15,000}{80,000} = £0.19$$

The Price Earnings Ratio is found by:

$$\frac{\text{Market price per share}}{\text{Earnings per share}} = \frac{£1.5}{£0.19} = 8$$

A price earnings ratio of 8 is fairly low but it should be compared with the ratio for other firms in the same industry.

Profitability Ratio—Profit to Capital Employed

It is probably true to say that this should be the first ratio which the financial analyst or investor calculates, as it may be said to be the ultimate test of business efficiency. It forms the basis of the pyramid structure of ratios used by the Centre for Interfirm Comparisons and is known as the primary ratio.

The term capital employed is unfortunately subject to many different interpretations. We have already considered one interpretation earlier in this chapter, i.e. equity capital plus retained earnings. When using it to form a measure of profitability it is usual to calculate it by taking the current liabilities from the total assets. More, however, will be said about this important ratio in the next chapter, as it forms an important part of management control by ratios.

Profit is also subject to controversy. Should the profits used in the calculation be before or after tax? Those in favour of using a net profit figure after tax claim that it represents a more realistic figure of the amount available for financing and remunerating the capital. Those supporting the net profit before tax concept point out that their profit figure gives a fairer indication of the actual performance of the assets which have been utilised to produce the profit. Also the tax charge of each company is affected by individual circumstances, e.g. variations in capital allowances or even by differing skills in taxation management. Tax rates are subject to change from period to period, making comparisons over such periods difficult if tax is taken into account in the return on capital employed computation.

We shall produce both versions from our figures.

1. Return on capital employed (after tax).

$$\frac{\text{Profit (after tax)}}{\text{Assets} - \text{Current liabilities}} = \frac{£18,000}{£260,000} - £40,000$$

$$= \frac{£18,000}{£220,000} \times \frac{100}{1} = 8 \cdot 2\%$$

2. Return on capital employed (before tax)

$$\frac{\text{Profit}}{\text{Assets} - \text{Current liabilities}} = \frac{£35,000}{£220,000} \times \frac{100}{1} = 15 \cdot 9\%$$

The significance of these figures will be considered in the next chapter. However, it might be said here that if a reasonable rate of return cannot be earned on the capital, then it would be better employed elsewhere.

There is a direct relationship between the rate of return on capital employed and the ratio of net profit to sales. We calculated this ratio earlier in this chapter to be 9·6%.

The net assets (i.e. Assets − Current liabilities) have generated £365,000 of sales or have turned over $\frac{£365,000}{£220,000}$ = 1·66 times.

If we now link these two ratios, i.e. 1·66 × 9·6% we have the return on capital employed of 15·9% originally calculated.

Conclusion

Ratio analysis has a number of limitations which have already been considered, and ratios in themselves cannot provide answers for management or investors; but they do highlight trends and allow comparisons to be made, and when applied intelligently can be a valuable tool.

Questions

1. Explain what you understand by the term "overtrading".
2. How is the "quick ratio" or "acid test" ratio calculated and what is its significance?
3. Explain the importance of the proprietor's ratio.
4. A firm has a gearing ratio of 4 : 1; is it high- or low-geared, and what is the significance of gearing?
5. Give the formula for calculating the average period in which debtors pay their accounts.
6. What factors are likely to affect the gross profit ratio?
7. How is the dividend yield calculated?
8. What is the importance of the price/earnings ratio?
9. Outline the advantages and disadvantages of calculating the return on capital employed using the profit before tax is deducted.
10. What are the limitations of ratio analysis?

Chapter 10

UNIFORM COSTING AND INTERFIRM COMPARISONS

Uniform Costing

Uniform costing is defined as "the use by several under-takings of the same costing principles and/or practices".

It is most usefully employed by large business organisa-tions which have a number of factories spread over a wide area, manufacturing the same type of product under similar conditions or operating the same type of service. It may also be used by trade associations when processes are standardised and easily identifiable.

The concept of uniform costing is not a new one; indeed the first scheme using such a system was introduced in the United States of America at the end of the last century. Perhaps the most famous scheme in Britain is that of the Federation of Master Printers which was first operated in 1913; and since then a number of other industries have used the technique.

In order to ensure that uniform costing will be of value, it is first necessary to establish that comparisons between different firms in an industry are in fact possible. This means that the following matters will have to be con-sidered:

(a) the type of costing system to be used (i.e. con-tract, job, batch or process costing, or some combination if that is more suitable);

(b) the methods of overhead recovery;

(c) the methods of depreciation;

(d) the definition of terms such as direct costs and indirect costs;

(e) the designing of a suitable cost classification coding system;

(f) the system of stores pricing and valuation of year-end stocks and work in progress, including the treat-ment of scrap and obsolete stores;

(*g*) the design of suitable statement forms which can be easily completed from existing records;

(*h*) the methods of remunerating labour including standard bonus schemes;

(*i*) a standard unit of production;

(*j*) the inclusion of charges for rent and interest on capital, even though premises for example are actually owned by the concern.

The technique of uniform costing is not just restricted to industrial concerns. Local authorities for example have a comprehensive system of cost comparisons for different services by which one local authority is able to compare the cost of a service (e.g. Housing, Education, Police, etc.) with all the other major authorities in the country. The information is produced by the Institute of Municipal Treasurers and Accountants and the Society of County Treasurers on an annual basis; and a standard accounting system is recommended by the former body to ensure that the costs are compiled on an equitable basis and can in fact be compared.

The advantages of uniform costing are:

1. Constant attention will be paid to the best methods of ascertaining and presenting cost data within the particular industry.

2. Better operating efficiency is possible because of the stimulation of the competitive spirit and a deeper understanding of the role of costing and of its value to the organisation.

3. Components and materials can be standardised, and pricing policies may be determined on a more realistic basis.

The main difficulties are:

1. The problem of standardisation of terms is not easy to overcome as the methods and needs of each firm will be different.

2. The adaptation of a firm's present costing system to suit a standard costing system may be expensive.

3. It is often difficult to persuade firms to disclose confidential information to the central collection agency, for fear that it will be disclosed to competitors.

4. There are many factors which affect different firms in different ways. For example, geographical location of the firm may increase or reduce its costs; or the available supply of labour may affect decisions on mechanisation and automation.

Tremendous interest has been shown in the establishment of uniform costing over a wide field of industrial activities since the Centre for Interfirm Comparisons began in 1959. The work of the Centre is described below.

Interfirm Comparisons

(The author wishes to acknowledge with thanks the help given by the Centre for Interfirm Comparison in the preparation of this section. Most of the material was supplied by the Centre.)

An interfirm comparison scheme is intended to show the management of each firm taking part how its profitability and productivity compares with that of other firms in the same industry; in what respects the firm is weaker or stronger than its competitors; and what specific questions of policy or performance should be tackled if the firm's profitability and productivity are to be raised.

In 1959 an organisation known as the Centre for Interfirm Comparison Limited was set up by the British Institute of Management in association with the British Productivity Council, to meet the demand of industry and trade for an expert body to conduct interfirm comparisons on a confidential basis as a service to management. It was established as a separate company, although it is a non-profit-making organisation, in order that its services should not be confined to members of its sponsoring organisations but made widely available to industry and trade. The major aims of the Centre are:

1. To offer a special service to trade associations, acting on their behalf as a "neutral" expert organisation for the promotion and conduct of interfirm comparisons among their members.

2. To undertake interfirm comparisons by direct arrangement with individual firms.

3. To run seminars on management ratios and interfirm comparison—some of a general nature, and others designed for particular industries and trades.

4. To carry out research aimed at making the best methods of interfirm comparison available to British industry and trade.

5. To offer its international connections to British firms wishing to compare their efficiency and costs with their opposite numbers in such countries as Germany, France, Switzerland, Holland, Belgium and the United States.

Independent External Yardstick

There are three standards by which to measure the performance of a firm—its past performance; budgets; and interfirm comparisons. Comparisons with the past have the disadvantage that the economic climate and the state of technology is constantly changing. It is therefore impossible to know with certainty whether a change over time is due to a change in efficiency or to economic and technological changes. The disadvantage of comparisons with budgets is that even the best budgets depend on the estimates of the executives who compile them, with all the limitations that such an approach implies.

With interfirm comparisons there is the outstanding advantage that a comparison is made between the performance of a firm with that of other firms operating in the same competitive conditions during the same period of time. Interfirm comparisons therefore provide an independent external yardstick against which to assess the performance of a company.

In theory, there are two possible approaches to the conduct of an interfirm comparison—by using the services of such organisations as the Centre, or by "doing-it-yourself". The major drawback of the "do-it-yourself" approach is its reliance on published information from other companies. The Centre estimates, for instance, that only 10–20% of the information used in its comparisons could be calculated from published accounts, and that even this information is unlikely to have been arrived at on a comparable basis. A further disadvantage inherent in the use of published information is that the terminology, the definitions and the valuation principles of different accountants are not standard. Divisions of large organisations do not have to publish accounts and it has been estimated that about 75% of all limited companies are exempt, under the Companies Act 1967, from disclosing some of the information required by that act. Few firms take account of an inflation factor in their published data, and it is well known that the once-a-year balance sheet may be drawn up at a time which is not typical of the year as a whole. All these disadvantages are avoided in a properly organised interfirm comparison.

Individual Report

A comparison organised by the Centre goes through a number of stages. First, a group of firms, which are sufficiently comparable and sufficiently numerous to make a comparison between them worth while, is built up by the Centre, usually acting with the close co-operation of the relevant trade associations. In many comparisons the next stage is to visit each of the participating firms to discover more about its mode of operating, and to find out what information about its activities it can readily provide.

With this information, the staff of the Centre will then devise a set of ratios which, on the one hand provides the firms with the information that they want, while on the other hand does not put inordinate demands upon the accounts and other departments to provide the necessary basic information. The Centre then sends a questionnaire to participating firms which provides all the information required when completed. As well as the questionnaire, participants are sent definitions of all terms used so that each can be sure that the figures have been arrived at on a strictly comparable basis. When the questionnaires are returned to the Centre they are checked and, if necessary, the figures are amended after discussion with the firms concerned.

A general report is then prepared and sent to each participating firm. This report will contain all the ratios for each firm, together with background information which enables the participant to compare his firm with those firms most similar to his own. If there are general conclusions to be drawn from the figures as a whole, these are incorporated in this report.

Senior members of the Centre's staff then write an individual report which interprets for each individual participant the conclusions which it seems he should draw from the figures in the general report. Often these reports are then discussed at follow-up meetings at the firm between members of their top management team and senior personnel from the Centre.

Confidentiality and Cost

The Centre is completely independent and no information supplied to it by companies is passed to any other organisation. The results of interfirm comparisons are made available to participating companies only. In the reports, the comparative data showing the figures for participating firms do not, of course, appear under the name of the firm, but under code numbers. The data are expressed in ratio, percentage and similar statistical forms (rather than as absolute figures), which reduces the possibility of identification.

It is impossible to quote in advance a price for the service because it will vary according to the amount of time and expense incurred in building up the comparison group, the amount of detail to be covered by the comparison, whether firms need to be visited (for example, to discuss the arrangements for, or the results of, the comparison), and the amount of individual written interpretation provided. However, for each comparison scheme a definite fee is quoted before companies are asked to commit themselves to participate.

Existing Schemes

It was stated above that the first stage of a comparison was to build up a group of participants. However, in many industries such groups already exist, and interested firms can therefore expect to receive the results of comparisons that much sooner.

The following list shows the industries and trades in which the Centre for Interfirm Comparison has prepared or is preparing IFC schemes:

Bedding manufacture
Biscuit manufacture
Blanket manufacture
Book publishing
Building and civil engineering
Cable trunking manufacture
Carpet manufacture
Central heating manufacture
Chemical manufacture *
"C" licence vehicle operating
Clothing manufacture
Cold-rolled sections
Colour makers
Cotton spinning
Confectionery manufacture
Corn and agricultural merchants
Crane manufacture
Distribution
Distributors of electronic calculators
Drop forgers
Dyers and finishers
Electrical contractors
English woollen and worsted industry
Flexible packaging
Flexible packaging manufacture
Food manufacture
Forgemasters
Footwear manufacture
Fork-lift truck manufacture
Furniture warehousing and removing
Gauge and tool manufacture
Glass container manufacture
Hand-tool manufacture
Insurance brokers

Joinery manufacture
Leather dressing
Light engineering *
Machine-tools manufacture
Mains cable manufacture
Maltsters
Medium/heavy engineering *
Narrow fabric manufacture
Nylon hose dyeing
Painting and decorating contractors
Paper manufacture
Periodical publishers
Pharmaceutical manufacture
Pipework contractors
Plastics trade moulding
Pump manufacture
Radio and electronic component manufacture
Rayon weaving
Road haulage:
  (a) Bulk liquid haulage contractors
  (b) Express carriers
Rubber manufacture *
Scientific instrument manufacture
Scottish woollen industry
Shirt manufacture
Soft drinks manufacture
Steel stockholders
Stockbrokers
Structural steelwork (fabrication and erection)
Synthetic resin manufacture
Tank and industrial plant contractors

* Covering various types, sizes and product groups.

Throwsters   Tufted carpet manufacture
Timber engineers   Valve manufacture (industrial)
Timber importers   Warp knitting
Timber merchants

An Example of IFC

The following is a much condensed example of an IFC in a
light engineering industry. In the actual comparison about
thirty-five firms took part. Some forty ratios with a considerable amount of background information were provided to participants. The "pyramid" of ratios presented
on page 131 shows the set of the *major* management ratios
covered by the IFC, and explains why the individual
ratios were chosen.

The ratio of operating profit/operating assets is selected
as the primary ratio because it reflects the earning power of
the operations of a business. A favourable ratio will indicate that a company is using its resources effectively,
and will put it into a strong competitive position.

The relationship between a firm's operating profit/
operating assets depends first of all on two other important
relationships (ratios)—namely that between its operating
profit and its sales, and that between its sales and its
operating assets.

Ratio 2 shows *what* profit margin has been earned on
sales, while ratio 3 shows *how often* the margin has been
earned on assets in the year. Ratio 3 shows how many
times assets have been turned over in a year. Ratio 3a
indicates the assets required per £1,000 of sales.

Thus the return on operating assets of a firm depends on
the relationship between its ratios 2 and 3, and this in
turn depends on the relationships between its sales and
its profits (and therefore its costs), and between its sales
and its assets.

Table 1, on page 132, shows the ratios of a light engineering firm for two years.

This looks like a success story: return on assets (ratio 1)
has gone up from 8·7 to 10·8% due to a rise in both the
firm's profit on sales (ratio 2) and its turnover of assets
(ratio 3). The former has improved because the fall in the
firm's production cost ratio 4 has been greater than the

'PYRAMID' OF RATIOS FOR GENERAL MANAGEMENT

Copyright of
"Centre for Interfirm Comparisons"

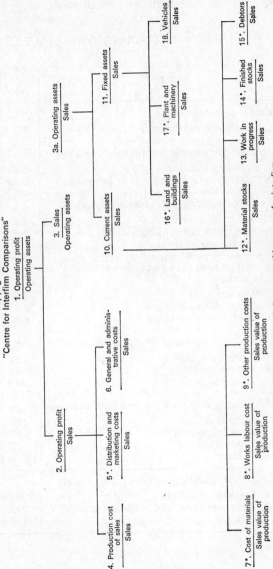

* Explanatory ratios relating to possible reasons for interfirm differences in these ratios are used in an actual comparision.

TABLE 1—THE FIRM'S OWN FIGURES

Ratios	Last year	This year
Return on assets		
1. Operating profit/Operating assets (%)	8·7	10·8
Profit margin on sales and turnover of assets		
2. Operating profit/Sales (%)	8·9	10·7
3. Sales/Operating assets (times per year)	0·97	1·01
Departmental costs (as percentage of sales)		
4. Production cost of sales	77·4	75·4
5. Distribution and marketing costs	4·6	4·9
6. General and administrative costs	9·1	9·0
Production costs (as a percentage of sales value of production)		
7. Materials costs	34·7	33·1
8. Works labour costs	27·4	26·8
9. Other production costs	15·3	15·5
General asset utilisation (£s per £1,000 of sales)		
3a. Operating assets	1,031	990
10. Current assets	582	549
11. Fixed assets	449	441
Current asset utilisation (£s per £1,000 of sales)		
12. Material stocks	101	100
13. Work in progress	215	188
14. Finished stocks	53	44
15. Debtors	213	217
Fixed asset utilisation (£s per £1,000 of sales)		
16. Land and buildings	206	201
17. Plant, machinery and works equipment	237	233
18. Vehicles	6	7

rise in its marketing and distribution cost ratio 5. Ratio 4 in turn has improved as a result of falls in the firm's material and works labour cost ratios 7 and 8.

As to the firm's asset utilisation ratios, there has been an improvement on both the current and fixed asset sides (ratios 10 and 11). The rise in the debtors ratio 15 is more than off-set by falls in the materials stock, work-in-progress and finished-stock ratios 12, 13 and 14. Furthermore, the two major fixed asset investment ratios 16 and 17 have improved.

But the firm's illusion of success was shattered when it compared its ratios with those of other light engineering firms of its kind. Table 2, on page 134, is an extract from the results—it gives the figures of only seven of the thirty-five participating firms. Our firm's figures are shown under letter E.

As Table 2 shows, this year the firm's profit on assets is well below that of four other firms and this is due to both its profit on sales (ratio 2) and turnover of assets (ratio 3) being relatively low. The firm's profit on sales (ratio 2) is relatively low mainly because both its production cost ratio 4 and its general and administrative cost ratio 6 are comparatively high, even though they compared well with the firm's previous year's figures. Firm E's distribution and marketing cost ratio 5 on the other hand, which had risen during the last year, is the lowest of all; this might reflect an insufficient marketing effort. The firm's production cost ratio 4 is comparatively high because although its materials and works labour cost ratios 7 and 8 have improved, it now turns out that both these ratios, and also its other production costs' ratio are higher than those of firms A to D.

As to the utilisation of current asset investment, the firm's work-in-progress ratio 13 is higher (i.e. less favourable) than those of firms A to D, even though it had improved in comparison with the previous period. Its finished stock investment ratio 14, on the other hand, is almost the lowest of all; this, however, is not necessarily a favourable indication, since greater emphasis on stock production of standard products or components might help the firm to manufacture more economically.

TABLE 2—THE INTERFIRM COMPARISON

Ratios	A	B	C	D	E	F	G
Return on assets							
1. Operating profit/ Operating assets (%)	25·1	23·9	18·9	13·2	10·8	4·3	3·5
Profit margin on sales and turnover of assets							
2. Operating profit/ Sales (%)	19·0	19·9	15·1	11·5	10·7	4·7	3·6
3. Sales/Operating assets (times per year)	1·32	1·20	1·25	1·15	1·01	0·92	0·98
Departmental costs (as a percentage of sales)							
4. Production cost of sales	62·8	63·5	71·1	71·9	75·4	80·2	80·9
5. Distribution and marketing costs	11·4	12·6	6·6	6·9	4·9	5·6	6·1
6. General and administrative costs	6·8	4·0	7·2	9·7	9·0	9·5	9·4
Production costs (as a percentage of sales value of production)							
7. Materials costs	32·0	28·7	32·9	31·6	33·1	35·8	33·8
8. Works labour costs	16·5	22·1	24·2	25·1	26·8	28·9	29·2
9. Other production costs	14·3	12·7	14·0	15·2	15·5	15·5	17·9
General asset utilisation (£s per £1,000 of sales)							
3a. Operating assets	758	833	800	864	990	1,081	1,016
10. Current assets	465	481	412	474	549	608	543
11. Fixed assets	293	352	388	390	441	473	473
Current asset utilisation (£s per £1,000 of sales)							
12. Material stocks	80	110	71	92	100	102	96
13. Work in progress	43	40	63	101	188	215	220
14. Finished stocks	132	102	57	75	44	67	19
15. Debtors	210	229	221	206	217	224	208
Fixed asset utilisation (£s per £1,000 of sales)							
16. Land and buildings	130	158	194	174	201	244	241
17. Plant, machinery and works equipment	160	189	190	213	233	220	225
18. Vehicles	3	5	4	3	7	9	·7

The firm's fixed asset investment ratio 11 is comparatively unfavourable, mainly because both its land and buildings ratio 16 and its plant investment ratio 17 (which had improved) are considerably higher than those of firms A to D.

In the actual IFC, firm E received a detailed report relating both to the above ratios and the additional ratios mentioned at the foot of page 131 ; discussing the policy and performance factors underlying the firm's position in the IFC; highlighting its weaknesses and strengths, and indicating the directions in which improvements should be made.

What Does This Example Show ?

IFC—A Better Basis for Judgment. Comparisons between two years may create a feeling of false security. Only an interfirm comparison could show that the results achieved by this firm were not good enough.

IFC—A Guide to Action. Our firm can draw specific conclusions from the comparison because the figures compared were carefully selected with a definite plan in mind : it was known that the comparative figures were wanted by managing directors as an aid in the overall direction of their businesses. Accordingly, ratios were chosen which would indicate to each firm how its return on capital compared with that of the others, and to help those with a comparatively low return on capital to narrow down systematically the possible reasons for this. Aided by the Centre's report, our firm will now investigate the reasons why its production costs, work-in-progress and plant-investment ratios are relatively unfavourable.

IFC—Ratios Express Key Relationships. Ratios are used for comparison because they provide a better basis for judgment than their underlying figures. For instance, a firm may make a hundred of its products in one month and a hundred and twenty in the subsequent month. This is a sign of improvement *only if* the costs of the resources used in making these products have not increased at the same or even a higher rate. Only ratios can express this relationship between output and resources used, and other key relationships of importance to management.

IFC—Security. Clearly ratios such as those used in the example do not disclose the actual figures of participating firms. A firm's sales may have been £100,000 with a capital of £50,000, or £20,000 with a capital of £10,000; but in either case its ratio of sales to capital will be 2:1 or its "turnover" of capital two times.

On page 137 you will find an alternative presentation of interfirm comparison.

What the Comparison Shows Firm 6

Suppose you are the managing director of firm 6 in the table shown on page 137, what does the comparison show you?

1. First and most important, the comparison gives you for the first time an objective yardstick of your firm's overall success—as indicated by the standing of your operating profit/operating assets ratio against that of other firms.

The comparison of this primary ratio shows that your firm's overall success and effectiveness is *less* than that of the majority of the others, since your return on assets is only 7·9% against the median of 11·3%.

2. What is the cause of your low operating profit/operating assets? Comparison of ratios 2 and 3 shows that the reason is your low operating profit/sales—your figure of 6·1% is the third lowest of the figures shown. On the other hand, your turnover of assets, ratio 3, is the fastest of any firm. It therefore seems that you should first of all investigate the cost ratios which determine your operating profit/sales.

3. Looking at the departmental cost ratios, you find that your production cost, ratio 4, is high; your distribution and marketing cost, ratio 5, is below-average; and your administration cost, ratio 6, is above-average.

4. The causes of your high ratio 4 are shown by ratios 7 and 8 to be your high materials and labour costs. In the actual comparison, you have access to more detailed comparative data which throws further light on these

AN ALTERNATIVE PRESENTATION OF INTERFIRM COMPARISON

Ratios	1	2	3	4	5	6	7	8	9	Median*
1. Operating profit/Operating assets	20·2	17·9	14·3	13·3	11·3	7·9	7·4	3·9	3·1	11·3
2. Operating profit/Sales	18·2	14·9	13·1	11·9	10·9	6·1	7·6	3·1	3·8	10·9
3. Sales/Operating assets (times)	1·11	1·20	1·09	1·12	1·04	1·30	0·98	1·25	0·81	1·11
Departmental Costs (as a percentage of sales)										
4. Production costs	71·3	77·1	77·4	79·6	79·4	84·2	82·5	89·5	84·3	79·6
5. Distribution and marketing costs	4·9	3·7	4·1	2·2	3·3	2·9	4·4	3·3	3·6	3·6
6. Administrative costs	5·6	4·3	5·4	6·3	6·4	6·8	5·7	4·1	8·3	5·7
Production costs (as a percentage of sales value of production)										
7. Materials cost	46·9	53·0	51·0	50·8	56·2	55·3	56·3	56·5	51·7	53·0
8. Works labour cost	10·4	9·8	7·3	10·1	9·2	12·3	8·2	16·1	14·7	10·1
9. Production overheads	14·0	14·3	19·1	18·7	14·0	16·6	18·0	16·9	17·9	16·9
Asset utilisation (£s per £1,000 of sales)										
3a. Total operating assets	899	833	918	893	960	770	1,019	798	1,233	899
10. Current assets	328	384	400	351	379	404	589	423	430	400
11. Fixed assets	571	449	518	542	581	366	430	375	803	518
Current asset utilisation (£s per £1,000 of sales)										
12. Material stocks	58	73	43	58	86	65	129	80	68	68
13. Work in progress	51	90	104	63	44	114	164	122	135	104
14. Finished stocks	66	94	123	63	118	77	147	60	84	84
15. Debtors	153	127	130	167	131	148	149	161	143	148
Fixed asset utilisation (£s per £1,000 of sales)										
16. Land and buildings	240	87	102	143	156	88	47	73	299	102
17. Plant and machinery	316	343	407	389	413	267	363	289	486	363
18. Vehicles	15	19	9	10	12	11	20	13	18	13

Firms

* The median is the middle figure for each ratio

points—it shows (*a*) that your high materials cost is
related to your high materials waste ratio, and (*b*) that
your high works labour cost is caused, not by high wages,
etc. costs per employee, but by low volume of output per
employee.

5. Turning to the asset utilisation ratios you see that your
fast turnover of total operating assets (ratio 3) is expressed
in a different way by ratio 3a, which shows that you have
the lowest figure of tota operating assets per £1,000 of
sales. You will see from ratio 11 that this is because you
have the lowest figure of fixed assets in relation to sales.
This is, in turn, mainly due to your low plant and machinery
ratio (ratio 17). Incidentally, the fixed asset figures used
in this comparison are based upon comparable valuations.

The more detailed data available (not shown in this
table) indicate that the average age of your plant is
greater than that of most other firms; and that your value
of plant and machinery per works employee is below the
average. The comparison therefore suggests that your
low labour productivity (a major cause of your high production costs) may be due to the fact that your plant is
not sufficiently up-to-date.

6. Your current asset utilisation ratios (ratios 12 to 15)
show that most of your current asset items are about
average—with the exception of your work-in-progress,
ratio 13, which is above the average. This seems to provide
another indication of the need for altering your production
arrangements so as to allow a faster throughput.

*Summary: The Scope for Improvement, Measured in
Ratios and Absolute Figures.* If you were able to achieve
materials and labour cost ratios equal to the medians,
while retaining your present production overheads ratio
and the same ratios for your other departmental costs, your
profit to sales ratio would improve to 10·6%.

In order to achieve your improved labour cost ratio,
you might have to spend more on new plant. Supposing
you increased your plant value (which at the moment is
£267 per £1,000 of sales) by 50%, then your fixed assets
ratio would increase to £499. However, you should be
able to improve your works-in-progres figure to the

median, giving a lower current asset ratio (ratio 10) of
£394. Your rate of turnover of operating assets (ratio 3)
would then become 1·12 times. Because of your increased
investment in plant and machinery, your depreciation
would go up, and the effect of this would be to increase
your production overheads ratio to 17·6%; your profit
margin on sales would then become 9·6% and your
return on assets 10·8%—i.e. nearly three percentage
points higher than it is now.

In terms of absolute figures: your present sales volume
is £2 million. At the same volume of sales, your new profit
ratio would mean a profit of £192,000—an improvement
of £70,000 on your present profits.

Return on Capital Employed—Problems

We have already considered a number of problems in
connection with the definition of the term capital employed. Let us review the various possible definitions:

1. *Total Gross Capital Employed.* This is the sum of the
issued share capital, reserves, loans and current liabilities,
in other words the total fixed and current assets.

2. *Total Net Capital Employed.* This is the most popular
and acceptable definition. It can be found by either
adding together the share capital, reserves and loans or by
deducting current liabilities from total assets.

3. *Total Shareholders' Capital Employed.* This is
represented by the sum of issued capital plus reserves.

4. *Total Equity Capital Employed.* This is the sum of
issued ordinary share capital and reserves.

Which is the best definition to use is likely to depend
upon the purpose for which the capital employed figure
is to be used; but no matter how it is calculated there are
two important points to bear in mind.

First, as one is attempting to establish a rate of return on
the capital employed in the business, it is essential that all
the assets used for the calculation are in fact being usefully employed. For example, if a large cash balance has
been allowed to accumulate or there has been a sudden
influx of cash due to a share issue, such excessive

balances are obviously not being usefully employed in the business and until they are (for example, by the purchase of new plant or stocks), they should be excluded from the computation. If the second point considered below is also adopted, intangible assets such as goodwill must also be eliminated.

The second consideration is the value to be placed on the assets when calculating the return. The figures which appear in the balance sheet rarely reflect the true value of the fixed assets being employed. This is primarily due to the conservative approach of the financial accountant in valuing assets at the lower of cost or market value.

Consider a company whose balance sheet figures reveal that the net capital employed totals £100,000 and the net profit before tax is £20,000. This will give a rate of return on the capital employed of 20%, i.e.:

$$\frac{£20,000}{£100,000} \times \frac{100}{1} = 20\%$$

But assume that the assets include land which was purchased for £10,000 twenty-five years ago and is still shown at that figure in the balance sheet. Obviously the current value of the land will be much more than £10,000 and a conservative estimate might put the value at £100,000. This means that the real value of the capital employed by our company is at least £190,000. This has a drastic effect on the rate of return, reducing it from 20% to just over 10%.

It is essential, therefore, to use some method by which all the assets of a company can be measured at current values. This is not an easy task and more will be said about the problems involved in a later chapter but the usual solution is to revalue by using price index numbers. Although this is a solution, it is rarely adopted in practice and great care should be exercised when using published rates of return on capital employed to ensure that the basis for the calculation is known and deficiencies in the basis are noted.

Questions

1. Outline the main points to be considered before a uniform costing system can be established.

2. Exemplify the advantages and disadvantages of uniform costing.

3. What are the major aims of the Centre for Interfirm Comparison?

4. Outline the main drawbacks of the "do-it-yourself" approach to interfirm comparisons.

5. Show by means of a diagram the "pyramid" of ratios used by the Centre for Interfirm Comparison.

6. Prepare a report for the management of Firm F from the figures given in the table on page 134.

7. Explain the importance of the operating profit/operating assets ratio.

8. Define "total net capital employed".

9. Should goodwill be included in the figure for total net capital employed?

10. What matters should be borne in mind when comparing returns on capital employed obtained from published accounts?

Chapter 11

CAPITAL INVESTMENT APPRAISAL

The process of budgeting for capital expenditure decisions is a vital part of policy making and top management usually assumes direct responsibility for the authorisation of all but the smallest capital investment sums.

The main reasons why these decisions should be the concern of top management are:

1. The sums involved in capital investment are usually very substantial.

2. Once decisions have been made the resources of the firm are likely to be tied up for some considerable time in the particular project to which the capital investment relates.

3. The future of the firm may depend on a single investment decision and it may be very difficult to reverse the effects of a bad decision.

4. Capital budgeting is a long-term function and the farther into the future that plans are made the more uncertain are the results.

The Main Influences Affecting the Capital Investment Decision

These will fall into three main categories:

(a) the future net increase in income or the future net saving in costs;
(b) the net amount of the investment;
(c) a satisfactory rate of return.

All these categories are related and it is probably necessary for management to decide first the minimum rate of return which will be acceptable, rejecting at once any project which does not meet this rate.

An immediate difficulty is to decide what rate of return on the capital expenditure is acceptable. If the money has to be borrowed in order to finance the project, the rate of return should obviously be at least sufficient to finance the cost of such borrowings. It is, however, necessary to take account of the increased risk factor because we are dealing with the uncertain future. There are a number of factors which can turn an apparently successful investment project into a "white elephant" over a very short period. For example, technological innovation may make the investment obsolete, or there may be a change of fashion which can have similarly disastrous results on the firm's earnings. In these circumstances a company may decide to increase the cost of capital by a risk factor to obtain the minimum acceptable rate of return. A different factor may be used for different classes of investments.

From research into the subject it appears that a figure of about 17% before deduction of tax would be acceptable as an average rate of return.

Although it has been stated that capital expenditure should be capable of generating a satisfactory return this is not possible in all cases. Most firms undertake capital expenditure which will definitely not yield any direct monetary returns, e.g. the provision of a medical centre or sports pavilion. This type of project will, no doubt, benefit the firm indirectly by improving the morale of employees but the immediate effect on profits will be to reduce them. The returns from "normal" profitable projects must therefore be loaded with a factor which will offset the cost of the non-profit-earning projects.

Methods of Evaluating Investment Decisions

The appraisal of capital projects may take one of two forms or a combination of the two. The first and perhaps the simplest is to evaluate two or more alternatives, and then select the one which yields the highest return after taking into account individual circumstances relating to that particular decision (e.g. the chance of obsolescence). The second is to evaluate a single project from the point of view of overall profitability and the possibility of achieving an acceptable rate of return.

The principal methods employed for evaluating capital projects are explained below.

1. *Total Income Method* (rate of return on original investment). This involves expressing the total expected income from a project as a percentage of its capital cost.

Example:

Cost, £300,000
Depreciation to be at rate of 20%
Life of asset, five years
Annual income before depreciation

		£
Year 1		80,000
„	2	100,000
„	3	100,000
„	4	120,000
„	5	120,000
		£520,000

	£
Total Forecast income	520,000
Less Depreciation, i.e. 100%	300,000

Net income after providing depreciation £220,000

Total return on the original investment is:

$$\frac{£220,000}{£300,000} \times 100 = 73\%$$

To calculate an average return per annum, the average income per annum is found by:

$$\frac{£220,000}{5} = £44,000 \text{ per annum}$$

This gives an average return of

$$\frac{£44,000}{£300,000} \times 100 = 14 \cdot 7\%$$

It is now widely accepted that this method has many defects. It takes no account of time or the interest value of money, and it is based on a five-yearly average of income rather than actual income each year.

2. *Rate of Return on Average Investment.* This method makes some attempt to take account of the time element but its operation is open to question.

It is recognised that during the life of the asset, provision must be made for depreciation. As this involves no actual cash outlay it means that each year additional cash becomes available for reinvestment or for use as working capital.

The mechanics of the calculation involve dividing the original investment by two to give an average investment over the period, which assumes that the amount recovered in the form of depreciation will be used effectively in the business. In the above example this will give

$$\frac{£300,000}{2} = £150,000$$

The rate of return on average investment now becomes

$$\frac{£44,000}{£150,000} \times 100 = 29 \cdot 3\%$$

This rate will obviously be twice the previous rate since the cost of the original investment has been halved.

The only merits of these two methods of appraisal are that the method of calculation is simple and they permit the immediate elimination of any project which shows a lower rate of return than the business is earning on the rest of the capital employed. Some comparisons may be possible between different projects, but even these may be fallacious because of the different distributions of the income over the period.

3. *Pay Back Period.* This method attempts to measure the time it will take the expected income to equal the original cost of the investment. Once again no attempt is made to discount future income to present values.

Taking the figures already considered.

	Income before depreciation	Cumulative income
	£	£
Year 1	80,000	80,000
„ 2	100,000	180,000
„ 3	100,000	280,000)
„ 4	120,000	400,000∫

It will be seen that the whole cost of the original investment, i.e. £300,000, is recovered during the currency of year 4.

The main value of this method is again the question of elimination of projects with too long a pay-back period. All figures showing future income are of necessity estimates. The longer the period the more likely are the estimates to be unreliable. There is always the danger that in our fast-changing technical environment the investment may become obsolete long before its normal working life is over. Therefore the quicker the cost can be recovered the smaller the effect of obsolescence. Again, if the concern is likely to suffer from a shortage of cash, the quicker outlays are recovered the better the concern will be.

The main disadvantage of this method is that, if it is used in isolation, total earnings are ignored. This could mean that an investment was rejected in favour of another project because of an unfavourable pay-back period, when in fact its *total earnings* might be much higher, over the expected life of the asset.

4. *Discounted Cash Flow.* The main drawback with all the methods so far considered is that no account has been taken of the fact that future income is worth less than income received today. The concept has nothing to do with inflation reducing the value of money, but with the fact that a person who foregoes spending money immediately expects to receive a reward for his action. This reward takes the form of interest.

CAPITAL INVESTMENT APPRAISAL

Consider an investment made today of £100 which is to receive interest at 5% per annum. The value of this investment in twelve months' time will therefore be:

	£
Original investment	100
One year's interest	5
	£105

In two years' time the value of the investment will be:

	£
Value at end of Year 1	105
Add One year's interest at 5% p.a. on £105 =	5·25
Value at end of Year 2	£110·25

This addition of 5% interest each year to the balance at the beginning of the year is known as compounding.

Let us now look at the opposite side of the coin. If a sum of £105 is to be received in twelve months' time, then if it is discounted at 5% p.a. the present value of that £105 is £100, viz.:

	£
Value in twelve months' time	105
Less 5% discount	5
Present value	£100

It should be noted that the rate of discount in the above example is really 4·71%. This is because, in practice, to discount £105 by 5% does not mean take £105 and deduct 5% from it but rather to decide the sum which, if invested now at 5% will produce £105 in one year's time. This will become clear when the formula for calculating the present value of a future sum is considered below.

It has already been mentioned that, when using compound interest, if the value of the £100 is required in two years' time, then the 5% is applied not only to the principal but also to the interest earned after the first year.

The initial interest amount is found by the formula:

$$1 + \frac{R}{100}$$

where R = rate of interest, i.e.:

$$1 + \frac{5}{100} = 1 \cdot 05$$

The standard formula for calculating compound interest is:

$$A = P \left(1 + \frac{R}{100}\right)^n$$

when A = amount, P = principal, R = rate of interest and n = number of years.

The present value of a £ due in twelve months' time is found by using the reciprocal of the first formula:

i.e. $$\frac{1}{1 \cdot 05} = 0 \cdot 952.$$

To obtain the present value of a future sum the formula is:

$$V = \frac{1}{(1 + R)^n} \text{ or } (1 + R)^{-n}$$

i.e. the reciprocal of the second formula.

Consider £100 invested for three years at 5% per annum:

Rate of Interest

End of Year 1 £100 × 1·05 = £105
" " " 2 £100 × (1·05 × 1·05) = £110·25
" " " 3 £100 × (1·05 × 1·05 × 1·05) = £115·763

Using these figures the discounting factor for each year is:

$$\text{Year 1} \quad \frac{1}{1 \cdot 05} = 0 \cdot 952$$

$$\text{,, } 2 \quad \left(\frac{1}{1 \cdot 05}\right)^2 = 0 \cdot 907$$

$$\text{,, } 3 \quad \left(\frac{1}{1 \cdot 05}\right)^3 = 0 \cdot 864$$

If the figure of £110·25, i.e. the amount of £100 for two years at 5% is multiplied by the discounting factor for Year 2 we have 110·25 × 0·907 = £100, i.e. the original principal sum.

It is not necessary to work out the discounting factors each time as they can be found from tables similar to the ones produced at the end of this chapter.

(a) *The Discounted Rate of Return (or Yield)*. If it is desired to compare the rate of return of related investments, both the investment and the expected cash income should be on a present value basis.

In order to equate the cash income which it is expected will be generated by the investment with the cost of the investment, the income must be discounted at a suitable rate. The procedure for finding the suitable rate is on a trial and error basis involving the use of the tables at the end of this chapter.

Let us restate our original problem:

Cost of investment, £300,000

				£
Expected income Year 1				80,000
,,	,,	,,	2	100,000
,,	,,	,,	3	100,000
,,	,,	,,	4	120,000
,,	,,	,,	5	120,000
				£520,000

We shall first have to take an arbitrary rate of discount and apply it to the income for each year. (For this simple illustration it is assumed that all income is received at the end of each year, and that the expenditure is regarded as having been made on 31st December of the base year, i.e. Year 0.) Let us try a rate of 15%.

From the tables the multiplying factor for Years 1 to 5 at a rate of 15% is:

End of Year 1	0·870
„ „ „ 2	0·756
„ „ „ 3	0·658
„ „ „ 4	0·572
„ „ „ 5	0·497

We now apply these factors to the income for each year:

Year	Cash flow	Discounting factor 15%	Present value
	£		£
1	80,000	0·870	71,600
2	100,000	0·756	75,600
3	100,000	0·658	65,800
4	120,000	0·572	68,640
5	120,000	0·497	59,640
	£520,000		£341,280

As the original cost of the investment is £300,000 the rate of 15% is too low. Let us try 22%.

Year	Cash flow	Discounting factor 22%	Present value
	£		£
1	80,000	0·820	65,600
2	100,000	0·672	67,200
3	100,000	0·551	55,100
4	120,000	0·451	54,120
5	120,000	0·370	44,400
	£520,000		£286,420

A rate of 22% is obviously too high, so we now know that the rate lies somewhere between 15% and 22%. Let us try 20%.

Year	Cash flow	Discounting factor 20%	Present value
	£		£
1	80,000	0·833	66,640
2	100,000	0·694	69,400
3	100,000	0·579	57,900
4	120,000	0·482	57,840
5	120,000	0·402	48,240
	£520,000		£300,020

This is as near as we shall be able to get using whole number interest figures, which means that the discounted rate of return for our example is 20%. This may be compared with an alternative project to ascertain which will yield the better return, and all other things being equal the project yielding the highest return will be the one adopted.

(b) *The Excess Present Value.* An alternative form of calculation is possible if a minimum acceptable rate of return is laid down. If the cash income from each alternative project is discounted at the minimum rate of return, the project which yields the highest excess value (on a present value basis) is the most acceptable.

Let us assume that the required minimum rate of return before tax is 16%.

The present value is calculated as above.

Year	Cash flow	Discounting factor 16%	Present value
	£		£
1	80,000	0·862	68,960
2	100,000	0·743	74,300
3	100,000	0·641	64,100
4	120,000	0·552	66,240
5	120,000	0·476	57,120
	£520,000		330,720
		Less Cost	300,000
		Excess Present value	£30,720

The excess present value of alternative projects which also cost £300,000, would be computed at a rate of 16%; and if they were all less than £30,720 the above project would be adopted.

It is also possible to calculate an index which gives the present value of a capital project per £1 invested. This is known as the profitability index, and for the above project would be

$$\frac{£330,720}{£300,000} = 110\%$$

Those projects with the highest index are the most profitable. Any project with an index below 100 would not be profitable since the discounted cash flows would be less than the original investment.

Problems of D.C.F. The advantages of using a discounting technique over the older and less sophisticated methods are fairly easy to appreciate; but even so it has its own pitfalls of which the reader should be aware.

Problems arise when attempting to compare two projects which have either different lives or different capital outlays. Consider first the choice between two projects which have different lives.

Example 1: A and B are two projects each costing £1,000 but the cash flow from A occurs at the end of Year 1 and is £1,115. The cash flow from B occurs over three years at a rate of £416 per year.

The rate of return or yield calculation is as follows:

Year	Cash flow	Discounting factor	Present value
	£	A	£
		15%	
A 1	1,150	0·870	1,000
		B	
		12%	
B 1	416	0·893	372
2	416	0·797	332
3	416	0·712	296
			£1,000

If the yield method is used to assess the two alternatives, project A would appear to be the better alternative as it yields 15% as against project B's 12%.

Excess present value calculation:

Assume that the minimum acceptable rate of return is 10%—

Year	Cash flow		Discounting factor 10%	Present value	
	A	B		A	B
	£	£		£	£
1	1,150	416	0·909	1,014	378
2		416	0·826		344
3		416	0·751		312
				1,014	1,034
			Less Capital cost	1,000	1,000
			Excess Present value	£14	£34

With this method of evaluation, project B shows the better return, having an excess present value of £20 over that of A. A gives an excess present value of £14 over 1 year, B gives an excess present value of £34 over 3 years; the most appropriate choice, therefore, will depend on what use is to be made of the cash flows. The yield method is only valid if it is assumed that there are other opportunities available offering a return higher than the firm's cost of capital. The profitability index for the two alternatives is project A $\frac{£1,014}{£1,000}$ = 100·14% and project B $\frac{£1,034}{£1,000}$ = 100·34%, which again shows a preference for project B.

Example 2: A and B are two projects, A costing £3,000 and B £16,000. The cash flow from A for two years is £2,010 each year and from B £10,470 each year.

The yield calculation will reveal the following:

Year	Cash flow	Discounting factor	Present value
	£	A	£
		22%	
A 1	2,010	0·820	1,650
2	2,010	0·672	1,350
			3,000
		B	
		20%	
B 1	10,470	0·833	8,724
2	10,470	0·694	7,266
			15,990

I.e. approximately £16,000

According to the yield method project A is to be pre-ferred having a yield of 22% as against project B's 20%.

The excess present value method, applying our 10% required minimum, gives us the following:

Year	Cash flow		Discounting factor 10%	Present value	
	A	B		A	B
	£	£		£	£
1	2,010	10,470	0·909	1,811	9,432
2	2,010	10,470	0·826	1,660	8,648
				3,471	18,080
		Less Capital cost		3,000	16,000
		Excess Present value		£471	£2,080

Using this method, project B is obviously the better alternative.

However if we apply the profitability index to the two projects, project A has an index of 115% and project B 113%, indicating that project A is again to be preferred.

The profitability index will give a more accurate ranking of alternatives than both the yield and E.P.V. methods, provided that the annual cash flows from the alternative projects can be reinvested at the minimum rate of return.

Effect of Taxation on Investment Decisions

The evaluation of competing projects is concerned primarily with the movement of cash over the period of the investment. Basic accounting concepts of matching expenses with revenues, etc., do not enter into the decision. It is when cash is spent and when cash is received which is of prime importance.

These cash flows are affected by taxation timing in paying the appropriate tax on the cash inflows and receiving investment grants and capital allowances on the outflows.

Let us first review the parts of the present taxation structure which are relevant to our particular problem.

Corporation Tax. Companies pay this tax on their adjusted profits at the rate of 45% (1969). There is, however, a delay in paying the tax on the profits of a particular period, and payment is usually not made for several months after the profits have been made. Tax which is deducted from dividend payments (at the standard rate of income tax) must, however, be accounted for to the Inland Revenue within one month.

Investment Grants. These are cash grants paid by the Board of Trade to an individual, partnership or company in the manufacturing, extractive, or hotel and restaurant industries. Manufacturing will cover all the processes resulting in the finished article but will not include services. Different rates of grant apply to businesses in a development area, and the basic grants applicable from January 1966 are shown below:

	Normal grant %	Development area grant %
New plant and machinery (in manufacturing, etc.)	20	40
New ships (other than for fishing)	20	—
New computers	20	—
New buildings and structures	—	25
New scientific research equipment for a process which qualifies under the general headings	20	40

The grants will normally be paid about eighteen months after the relevant expenditure has been incurred, and they are repayable if conditions are not fulfilled within a three year period.

Initial Allowances. Where cash grants are not available it is usually possible to claim an initial allowance. This will cover second-hand assets, industrial buildings outside a development area, and new plant and machinery purchased by those categories of business unable to claim an investment grant. The allowance is for one year only, i.e. the year in which the asset is purchased, and is at the rate of 15% for buildings and 30% for second-hand plant and machinery.

Capital allowances are also allowed against tax in place of the depreciation provided by individual companies. These are calculated each year generally on the reducing balance method, the rates being 15, 20 and 25% on the outstanding balance for plant and machinery, etc., the actual rate depending on the type of equipment, and its life. The rate on industrial buildings is 4% but calculated on the original cost.

An example of how these allowances work is given below.

Assume that new plant is purchased by a firm outside a development district and the appropriate annual writing down allowance is 20%.

	£	£
Cost of Plant		2,000

Year 1

Deduct investment grant, 20%	400	
		1,600
Annual capital allowance at 20%		320 (at 45% = £144)
		1,280

Year 2

Deduct annual allowance on outstand-ing balance at 20%	256 (at 45% = £115)
	£1,024

Year 3—and so on

Let us now consider how these tax calculations affect the cash outflows and inflows. If we assume a year end to be the 31st March, the Corporation Tax on the profits of that year are payable in the following year, and so the reduction in tax payable due to capital allowances must also be one year later.

Assume our plant is now purchased by a firm in a development area and the rate of capital or annual allowance is 25%. For simplicity we will ignore the actual cash inflows and just show what allowances may be claimed against such inflows.

Year	Cash outflow	Investment grant 40%	Corporation tax relief at 45%	Total
	£	£	£	£
1	2,000	—	—	—
2	—	800	135	935
3	—	—	101	101
4	—	—	76	76

The Corporation Tax relief as shown in the above illustration is calculated as follows :

Year 1 allowance affecting cash flows in Year 2:

	£
Cost of plant	2,000
Deduct investment grant, 40%	800
	1,200
Capital allowance, 25%	300

£900 written-down value

Tax saved is therefore £300 at 45% = £135.

Year 2 allowance affecting cash flows in Year 3:

	£
Capital allowance, 25% (on £900)	225

Tax saving as above £225 at 45% = £101

£675 written-down value

Year 3 allowance is calculated in a similar manner.

If we now assume that his new plant brings in additional cash flow profits over four years of £1,500 for the first two years and £1,000 for the next two, after which the plant is scrapped and has no residual value, the evaluation of the project would be as follows:

1 Year	2 Cash flow	3 Tax at 45%	4 Tax saved by allowances	5 Net cash flow ((2 − 3) + 4)	6 Discount factor, 10%	7 Present value
1	1,500	—	—	1,500	0·909	1,364
2	1,500	675	*935	1,760	0·826	1,444
3	1,000	675	101	426	0·751	320
4	1,000	450	76	626	0·683	428
5	—	450	228	(−222)	0·621	(−138)

	3,418
Less Original cost	2,000
Excess Present value	£1,418

* *Note.* The maximum amount of tax which may be offset by allowances in any one year is normally limited to the actual tax payable in that year. If allowances are greater than the tax payable, the excess will be carried forward to the next period. However the investment grant is paid in cash rather than offset against tax due so the normal provisions do not apply.

The final figure is calculated as follows:

	£
Cost of plant	2,000
Less Investment grant	800
	£1,200

Capital allowances deducted:

	£	£
Accounting Year 1	300	
" " 2	225	
" " 3	169	
		694
Allowance still to be claimed		506

As the plant is scrapped in Year 4 the total allowances due on the plant may be reclaimed in that year. Therefore, the tax saving in Year 5 is £506 × 45% = £228.

The importance of using cash flows after taxation adjustments is that account can be taken of the different investment, initial and annual allowances which may be claimed for different types of asset. It is possible to have two projects each with the same life, capital outlay and cash inflows but which attract different tax allowances, so that one project shows a better net return than the other.

Questions

1. Outline the main reasons why capital expenditure decisions are usually the concern of top management.
2. What are the main influences affecting the capital investment decision?
3. List the main method of evaluating investment decisions.
4. Explain the advantages and disadvantages of the pay-back method of appraisal.
5. What do you understand by discounting cash flows?
6. What formula is used to prepare a discounting table?
7. Explain how the discounted rate of return or yield method is calculated.

[continued on page 162

PRESENT VALUE FACTORS—PRESENT VALUE OF £1

Year hence	4%	5%	6%	7%	8%	9%	10%	11%	12%	13%	14%	15%	16%
1	0·962	0·952	0·943	0·935	0·926	0·917	0·909	0·901	0·893	0·885	0·877	0·870	0·862
2	0·925	0·907	0·890	0·873	0·857	0·841	0·826	0·812	0·797	0·783	0·769	0·756	0·743
3	0·889	0·864	0·840	0·816	0·794	0·772	0·751	0·731	0·712	0·693	0·675	0·658	0·641
4	0·855	0·823	0·792	0·763	0·735	0·708	0·683	0·659	0·636	0·613	0·592	0·572	0·552
5	0·822	0·784	0·747	0·713	0·681	0·650	0·621	0·594	0·567	0·543	0·519	0·497	0·476
6	0·790	0·746	0·705	0·666	0·630	0·596	0·564	0·535	0·507	0·480	0·456	0·432	0·410
7	0·760	0·711	0·665	0·623	0·583	0·547	0·513	0·482	0·452	0·425	0·400	0·376	0·354
8	0·731	0·677	0·627	0·582	0·540	0·502	0·467	0·434	0·404	0·376	0·351	0·327	0·305
9	0·703	0·645	0·592	0·544	0·500	0·460	0·424	0·391	0·361	0·333	0·308	0·284	0·263
10	0·676	0·614	0·558	0·508	0·463	0·422	0·386	0·352	0·322	0·295	0·270	0·247	0·227
11	0·650	0·585	0·527	0·475	0·429	0·388	0·350	0·317	0·287	0·261	0·237	0·215	0·195
12	0·625	0·557	0·497	0·444	0·397	0·356	0·319	0·286	0·257	0·231	0·208	0·187	0·168
13	0·601	0·530	0·469	0·415	0·368	0·326	0·290	0·256	0·229	0·204	0·182	0·163	0·145
14	0·577	0·505	0·442	0·388	0·340	0·299	0·263	0·232	0·205	0·181	0·160	0·141	0·125
15	0·555	0·481	0·417	0·362	0·315	0·276	0·239	0·209	0·183	0·160	0·140	0·123	0·108
16	0·534	0·458	0·394	0·339	0·292	0·252	0·218	0·188	0·163	0·142	0·123	0·107	0·093
17	0·513	0·436	0·371	0·317	0·270	0·231	0·198	0·170	0·146	0·125	0·108	0·093	0·080
18	0·494	0·416	0·350	0·296	0·250	0·212	0·180	0·153	0·130	0·111	0·095	0·081	0·069
19	0·475	0·396	0·331	0·277	0·232	0·196	0·164	0·138	0·116	0·098	0·083	0·070	0·060
20	0·456	0·377	0·312	0·258	0·215	0·178	0·149	0·124	0·104	0·087	0·073	0·061	0·051

Year hence	17%	18%	19%	20%	22%	24%	25%	26%	28%	30%	35%	40%	45%
1	0·855	0·847	0·840	0·833	0·820	0·806	0·800	0·794	0·781	0·769	0·741	0·714	0·690
2	0·731	0·718	0·706	0·694	0·672	0·650	0·640	0·630	0·610	0·592	0·549	0·510	0·476
3	0·624	0·609	0·593	0·579	0·551	0·524	0·512	0·500	0·477	0·455	0·406	0·364	0·328
4	0·534	0·516	0·499	0·482	0·451	0·423	0·410	0·397	0·373	0·350	0·301	0·260	0·226
5	0·456	0·437	0·419	0·402	0·370	0·341	0·328	0·315	0·291	0·269	0·223	0·186	0·156
6	0·390	0·370	0·352	0·335	0·303	0·275	0·262	0·250	0·227	0·207	0·165	0·133	0·108
7	0·333	0·314	0·296	0·279	0·249	0·222	0·210	0·198	0·178	0·159	0·122	0·095	0·074
8	0·285	0·266	0·249	0·233	0·204	0·179	0·168	0·157	0·139	0·123	0·091	0·068	0·051
9	0·243	0·225	0·209	0·194	0·167	0·144	0·134	0·125	0·108	0·094	0·067	0·048	0·035
10	0·208	0·191	0·176	0·162	0·137	0·116	0·107	0·099	0·085	0·073	0·050	0·035	0·024
11	0·178	0·162	0·148	0·135	0·112	0·094	0·086	0·079	0·066	0·056	0·037	0·025	0·017
12	0·152	0·137	0·124	0·112	0·092	0·076	0·062	0·062	0·052	0·043	0·027	0·013	0·012
13	0·130	0·116	0·104	0·093	0·075	0·061	0·055	0·050	0·040	0·033	0·020	0·013	0·008
14	0·111	0·099	0·088	0·078	0·062	0·049	0·044	0·039	0·032	0·025	0·015	0·009	0·006
15	0·095	0·084	0·074	0·065	0·051	0·040	0·035	0·031	0·025	0·020	0·011	0·006	0·004
16	0·081	0·071	0·062	0·054	0·042	0·032	0·028	0·025	0·019	0·015	0·008	0·005	0·003
17	0·069	0·060	0·052	0·045	0·034	0·026	0·023	0·020	0·015	0·012	0·006	0·003	0·002
18	0·059	0·051	0·044	0·038	0·028	0·021	0·018	0·016	0·012	0·009	0·005	0·002	0·001
19	0·043	0·043	0·037	0·031	0·023	0·017	0·014	0·012	0·009	0·007	0·003	0·002	0·001
20	0·037	0·037	0·031	0·026	0·019	0·014	0·012	0·010	0·007	0·005	0·002	0·001	0·001

Formula:

$$\frac{1}{(1 + i)^n}$$

where i is the rate of interest expressed as a decimal and n the number of years.

8. The excess present value method of appraisal requires the use of an acceptable rate of return. What factors must be taken into account when such a rate is decided upon?

9. Consider the problems of using discounted cash flow methods of investment appraisal.

10. Outline the effects of taxation on cash flows.

Chapter 12

ACCOUNTING FOR PRICE-LEVEL CHANGES

If it is accepted that one of the purposes of maintaining accounting records is to provide management with the necessary information to enable it to plan and control current and future operations it follows that the information must be as up to date and relevant as possible.

The standard of measurement used in accounting is a monetary unit which possesses a given amount of purchasing power within a given period of time. Unfortunately, this measure does not remain constant with changes in time, unlike physical measures such as the ton or the metre. Changes in the value of money mean that it is inaccurate to add together monetary values which relate to different periods.

Over the last thirty years most countries have seen a general fall in the purchasing power of their monetary unit (e.g. the pound, dollar, franc, etc.). This phenomenon is known as inflation, and is due to various factors operating within the economy. Most people are well aware of the effects of this fall in the value of money from their personal experience. The housewife complains that she is unable to buy the same amount of groceries as she formerly used to be able to with a given sum of money. If you change your car every two years for a new model you are unlikely to be able to buy the same model for the price as you previously paid, and if you are a house-owner you know that the value of your house in terms of the price you could sell it for rises every year, even though you may do nothing by way of improvements to it. It is interesting to note that the value rises despite the fact that each year the house becomes one year older and therefore more of a liability to repair, etc.

It would, therefore, seem fairly obvious that to add £s spent in 1960 to £s spent in 1970 creates a meaningless total, but in effect this is what accountants do when recording the financial transactions of their organisation and when preparing the annual financial statements. Their reluctance to take account of price-level changes has been blamed on their traditional conservative attitude, but that is not to say that they are unwilling to consider the problem. A great deal of research has been devoted to the price-level problem, but many difficulties have been encountered. As far back as 1936 Henry Whitcombe Sweeney published his now famous book, *Stabilised Accounting* and many of his theories still form the basis of present research.

Let us consider at this stage two practical illustrations to show the problem being considered.

Illustration No. 1

Assume that a man decides to buy a car for hiring out. The cost of the car is £1,600 and he expects it to last three years, after which he will replace it with an identical model and receive £100 on the old car in part exchange. The car is to be depreciated on the straight line method, i.e. the net cost of the car is divided by the number of years life of the car. This will give in our case:

Total cost, £1,600 − Scrap value, £100 = Net cost, £1,500

Annual depreciation is therefore $\frac{£1,500}{3}$ = £500 per year.

If the annual earnings are £800, the owner's Balance Sheet will show at the end of the life of the car:

	£		£
Capital	1,600	Cash	2,400
Profit	800		
	£2,400		£2,400

Let us assume now that owing to increasing prices over the past three years the price of the same type of car is now £2,400. This means that he started three years ago with a hire car and no cash, and if he now replaces the hire car he will again have a hire car and no cash. If any of the £800 profit has been withdrawn and spent by the owner, then there will be insufficient cash available to buy the new car and a loan or additional personal capital will be required. It certainly seems that the profit as shown by the above balance sheet is suspect, but as long as accountants continue to charge depreciation on a historical cost basis any profits so calculated do not reveal the true position.

Illustration No. 2

Assume that two men have an investment of 1,000 shares each in Company A which they purchased on 1st January at a price of £1 per share. The price of the share rises during the year and on 31st December one of the men sells his shares in Company A and receives £2 per share, i.e. £2,000. He invests this sum on the same day in Company B. How will these investments be shown on the individual Balance Sheets by the accountant at 31st December? The man who retains his holding in Company A will only show £1,000 as an investment, i.e. the cost price of the shares. The man whose investment is now in Company B will however show £2,000, yet the real value of both investments in current terms is the same, i.e. £2,000.

If it is assumed that price-level changes should concern the accountant he is faced with the problem of establishing a basis upon which adjustments can be made. Is it possible to recognise price-level changes when preparing accounting statements, and should they be incorporated in the actual accounts or shown in a supplementary statement to the accounts?

It is very unusual to find a company which has applied full revaluation accounting (as it is frequently called) to all their accounting systems. Perhaps the most famous example of full revaluation accounting in practice is the accounts of Philips Electrical Industries (N. V. Philip's Gloeilamppenfabrieken), which have used such a system for a number of years.

It is true to say, however, that although full revaluation accounting is rare, partial revaluation accounting is now becoming widely accepted in the accountancy professions of European countries and the United States; and many more firms are using such a system each year as its attributes become more widely appreciated. In Britain the Institute of Chartered Accountants in England and Wales published a research study in 1968 entitled *Accounting for Stewardship in a Period of Inflation*, in which they say that "ultimately one might look forward to the converted accounts taking the place of the conventional accounts as a basis for reporting on stewardship . . .".

Methods of Accounting for Price-level Changes

The two most widely accepted approaches to the problem are:

    (*a*) conversion of historical costs to replacement costs;
    (*b*) application of index numbers to historical data.

Replacement Costs. It is essential that the Profit and Loss Account each year is charged with a figure for depreciation of the fixed assets. This represents the current cost of using the asset and as has been already mentioned, this charge is usually based on the original cost of the asset. If, however, the prices of such assets are rising year by year, the annual charge calculated on historical costs does not represent a true cost of using the asset. It also follows that if the depreciation charge is less than it should be, profits are being overstated. The answer lies in the use of replacement costs, i.e. ascertaining what the cost would be if the assets currently in use were to be replaced. The figures so obtained would then provide the sum which depreciation charges could be calculated for charging to the Profit and Loss Account. The difference between historical cost depreciation and replacement cost depreciation would be credited to a "Revaluation Reserve Account".

If replacement costs are taken to be actual current costs of specific assets this is likely to take many other things into consideration besides the fall in the value of the purchasing power of money. It is unlikely that a replacement will be exactly the same; modifications may have been made to the original model or it may have become obsolete. There is nothing wrong with using replacement costs as long as these factors are borne in mind. It may well be that if actual replacement costs are compared with revaluations made on an index basis the two calculations will differ considerably.

If full revaluation accounting is to be used it is probably better to apply standard index numbers, bearing in mind the limitations mentioned later.

Index Numbers. It is necessary to find a suitable measure which shows the changes both upwards and downwards in the value of money. One such measure utilises index numbers and most countries publish each year a Consumer Price Index which is used by the government to measure changes in the internal purchasing power of the monetary unit. It should be remembered that such an index represents an average of consumer prices, i.e. the prices paid by the average household for goods and services. Obviously there is little connection between the type of goods forming part of such an index and the items purchased by a manufacturing concern, but unless a specific index is to be computed for every item which the business purchases the Consumer Price Index is the most authoritative basis at present available as a measure of general price-level changes.

Compiling an Index. The Consumer Price Index is calculated by expressing current average prices in relation to a base period index of 100. For example, if the price index is 111 this signifies that prices on average are 11% higher than they were in the base year.

The Consumer Price Index published in Great Britain appears in the *National Income Blue Book* about August of the following year and this is supplemented by monthly figures known as the Index of Retail Prices which is published the month following the month to which the index relates. The two indices are not compiled on identical lines, but the Retail Price Index is capable of giving changes over the short-term if these are required. The present base period of the Consumer Price Index is 1963 (i.e. the index is shown as 100 for 1963), and the following figures show the changes which have occurred in the general price level since 1958:

1958	89·9
1959	90·8
1960	91·8
1961	94·5
1962	98·2
1963	100
1964	103·2
1965	108
1966	112·1
1967	115
1968	120

Armed with this sort of information one can convert past pounds into current pounds and can therefore express the value of assets, etc., in a common measure.

Let us consider a simple example to illustrate how the conversion is carried out. We shall use fictitious index numbers for the sake of simplicity.

A company has the following assets, all of which are depreciated on a straight-line basis:

land purchased in 1950 cost £20,000, depreciated at 1% per annum;
buildings purchased in 1955 cost £50,000, depreciated at 2% per annum;
plant and machinery purchased in 1965 for £10,000, depreciated at 10% per annum;
vehicles purchased in 1970 for £5,000, depreciated at 20% per annum.

The relevant index numbers are 1950, 100; 1955, 130; 1965, 200; 1970, 290; and 1972, 300.

In order to convert the original cost to a current value the following formula is used:

$$\frac{\text{Current year index}}{\text{Year of purchase index}} \times \text{Original cost}$$

If it was decided to carry out a first revaluation in 1972 we would apply the above formula to our figures thus:

Year of Purchase	Description	Original cost	Index formula	Current value in 1972
		£		£
1950	Land	20,000	$\frac{300}{100}$	60,000
1955	Buildings	50,000	$\frac{300}{130}$	115,385
1965	Plant and machinery	10,000	$\frac{300}{200}$	15,000
1970	Vehicles	5,000	$\frac{300}{290}$	5,173
		£85,000		£195,555

The amount of depreciation charged in the accounts will have been based on historical costs and by the end of 1972 will be:

Assets	Depreciation rate	No. of years	Total
	%		£
Land	1	23	4,600
Buildings	2	18	18,000
Plant and machinery	10	8	8,000
Vehicles	20	3	3,000
			£33,600

It is, however, necessary to charge depreciation on the current value of the assets rather than historical costs and this will give the following figures.

Asset	Depreciation rate	No. of years	Total
	%		£
Land	1	23	13,800
Buildings	2	18	41,544
Plant and machinery	10	8	12,000
Vehicles	20	3	3,105
			£70,449

This means that an additional amount of £70,449 −
£33,600 = £36,849, must be charged in the accounts to
bring the total depreciation charge on these assets up to
current values. N.B. depreciation is calculated as follows:

$$\text{Land } \frac{1}{100} \times £20,000 \times 23 \text{ years}$$

$$= £4,600 \text{ on historical cost}$$

and

$$\frac{1}{100} \times £60,000 \times 23 \text{ years}$$

$$= £13,800 \text{ on current cost}$$

a similar formula being used for the other assets.

It will be seen that the initial conversion to current values
is a complicated and onerous task, but once all the figures
have been converted it is relatively simple to keep them
up to date each year by applying the relevant index.

The actual book-keeping transactions to take account
of the revaluation in 1972 are shown below:

Land

	£		£
1950 Balance	20,000		
1972 Revaluation reserve account	40,000	1972 Balance c/d	60,000
	£60,000		£60,000

Buildings

	£		£
1955 Balance	50,000		
1972 Revaluation reserve account	65,385	1972 Balance c/d	115,385
	£115,385		£115,385

Plant and Machinery

	£		£
1965 Balance	10,000		
1972 Revaluation reserve account	5,000	1972 Balance c/d	15,000
	£15,000		£15,000

Vehicles

	£		£
1970 Balance	5,000		
1972 Revaluation reserve account	173	1972 Balance c/d	5,173
	£5,173		£5,173

Revaluation Reserve

	£		£
		1972 Land	40,000
		1972 Buildings	63,385
		1972 Plant and machinery	5,000
1972 Balance c/d	108,558	1972 Vehicles	173
	£108,558		£108,558

Depreciation Provision

	£		£	£
		1972 Balance before revaluation		
		Land	4,600	
		Buildings	18,000	
		Plant and machinery	8,000	
		Vehicles	3,000	
				33,600
		1972 Profit and loss account		
1972 Balance c/d	70,449	(additional depreciation)		36,849
	£70,449			£70,449

Profit and Loss Account

	£		£
1972 Depreciation provision on revaluation of fixed assets	36,849	1972 Net profit for year (assume)	80,000
Net profit after additional depreciation	63,151	Profit b/f from previous years	20,000
	£100,000		£100,000

It will be appreciated that the first year in which revaluation is carried out it is likely to have a major effect on profits for that year. It may well be that there is insufficient profit available to meet the cost of the additional depreciation caused by showing the assets at current values. If this is the case, the additional amount required must be charged against any revenue reserves which have been established.

The relevant items in the Balance Sheet for 1972 after the revaluation would appear as follows:

Balance Sheet as at 31st December 1972

			Estimated replacement cost	Revalued depreciation	Current net value
			£	£	£
Revaluation reserve	108,558	Land	60,000	13,800	46,200
Profit and loss account	63,151	Buildings	115,385	41,544	73,841
		Plant and machinery	15,000	12,000	3,000
		Vehicles	5,173	3,105	2,068

An the end of 1973 the assets will be valued using the 1973 index. Any differences will be added to or deducted from the revaluation reserve as appropriate and the depreciation for the year will again be based on the 1973 revalued figure for each asset.

Current Assets. The figures for current assets, i.e. stock, debtors and cash at the end of the year are already in terms of current values. For example, if a business possesses £200 in cash, then that is the current value of the money. Stocks, to be acceptable as being at current values, should be valued on the Last In, First Out Basis (L.I.F.O.), i.e. on the assumption that items received last will be issued first and therefore the latest prices paid are used in the valuation.

Intangible Assets. This classification covers such items as trade marks, patents and goodwill. Owing to the uncertainty in estimating a value for such items it is probably better to exclude them altogether from the revaluation, and also to write them out of the balance sheet (except perhaps for a nominal value) as quickly as possible.

Limitations. It is essential that revaluation is not regarded just as an exercise in figure manipulation. Only assets which actually do increase in value should be subject to revaluation to bring them up to current values. The asset after revaluation should reflect as far as possible the current economic worth to the business. It is of little use revaluing an item of plant on the basis of index numbers, if management know that the plant will be obsolete in twelve months' time.

Bearing these limitations in mind, it still seems that if management are to be given meaningful accounting information, then such information must be measured at current price levels. As at least one large organisation with world-wide interests has proved over a long period that full revaluation accounting is a practical concept, it is hoped that in the future the majority of companies will see the value of, and will use accounts which have been adjusted for, price-level changes.

Questions

1. In a period of inflation is there anything wrong with adding the pounds of one year to the pounds of a previous year?

2. Illustrate the problems which may be caused by failure to take account of price changes.

3. Which company has successfully operated revaluation accounting for a number of years?

4. What are the two most widely accepted methods of accounting for price-level changes?

5. Explain the part played by depreciation in the price-level problem.

6. What do you understand by the term "Consumer Price Index"?

7. Why should such an index be a suitable measure for revaluing plant, etc?

8. How is an index compiled?

9. What account should be opened in the books of a company to record the additional depreciation on assets due to rising prices?

10. Should intangible assets be included in the revaluation process?

BIBLIOGRAPHY

The following selected bibliography is classified under three broad headings but many of the books listed will cover more than the particular category under which they appear.

Title	Author	Publisher
Financial Accountancy		
An Introduction to Business Accounting for Managers	Hartly, W. C. F.	Pergamon Press
Business Accounting, Parts I and II	Wood, F.	Longmans
Advanced Accounts	Carter, R. N.	Pitman
Modern Accounting Theory	Backer	Prentice-Hall
Studies in Accounting Theory	Baxter and Davidson	Sweet & Maxwell
Basic Business Finance	Hunt, Williams and Donaldson	Irwin
Business Finance	Paish	Pitman
Financial and Managerial Accounting	Bierman	Macmillan
Analysis and Interpretation of Financial Statements	Fitzgerald	Butterworth
Accounting Theory	Hendrikson	Irwin
Financial Management	Chambers	Law Book Co.
Guide to Company Balance Sheets and Profit and Loss Accounts	Jones	Heffer & Sons Ltd.
Cost Accountancy		
Essential Accounting for Managers	Robson	Cassell & Co.
Cost Accounting and Costing Methods	Wheldon	Macdonald & Evans Ltd.
Principles of Cost Accountancy	Buyers and Holmes	Macdonald & Evans Ltd.
Cost Accountancy	Harper	Macdonald & Evans Ltd.

Title	Author	Publisher
Business Budgets and Accounts	Edey	Hutchinson
Studies in Costing	Solomons	Sweet & Maxwell
An Introduction to Budgetary Control, Standard Costing, Material Control, and Production Control	I.C.W.A.	I.C.W.A.
A Report on Marginal Costing	I.C.W.A.	I.C.W.A.
Cost and Management Accountancy for Students	Batty	Heinemann Educational Books Ltd.
Standard Costing	Batty	Macdonald & Evans Ltd.
Flexible Budgetary Control and Standard Costing	Evans-Hemming	Macdonald & Evans Ltd.
Cost Accounting. A Managerial Emphasis	Horngren	Prentice-Hall
Cost Accounting: Analysis and Control	Shillinglaw	Irwin
Managerial Cost Analysis	Fremgen	Irwin
Budgetary Control	Court	Sweet & Maxwell

Management Accountancy

Management Accounting	Anthony	Irwin
Accounting for Management Control	Horngren	Prentice-Hall
Management Accounting in Practice	de Paula	Pitman
Principles of Management Accountancy	Brown and Howard	Macdonald & Evans Ltd.
Management Accountancy	Batty	Macdonald & Evans Ltd.
Management Accounting	Harper	Macdonald & Evans Ltd.
Developments in Management Accountancy	Batty	Heinemann
Managerial Accounting: An Introduction	Bierman and Drebin	Macmillan
The Accountant in Management	Tricker	Batsford

Title	Author	Publisher
Accounting for Management, Planning and Control	Lynch	McGraw-Hill
Accounting for Industrial Management	Sidebottom	Pergamon Press
Investment Decisions and Capital Costs	Porterfield	Prentice-Hall
Accounting for Price-Level Changes, Theory and Practice	Gynther	Pergamon Press
Discounted Cash Flow	Wright	McGraw-Hill
Capital Budgeting and Company Finance	Merett and Sykes	Longmans
Investment Appraisal	H.M. Stationery Office	H.M.S.O.

INDEX